CONFRONTING ISLAMOPHOBIA IN EDUCATIONAL PRACTICE

edited by Barry van Driel

tb

Trentham Books

Stoke on Trent, UK and Sterling, USA

Trentham Books Limited
Westview House   22883 Quicksilver Drive
734 London Road   Sterling
Oakhill   VA 20166-2012
Stoke on Trent   USA
Staffordshire
England ST4 5NP

© 2004 Barry van Driel

First published 2004

British Library Cataloguing-in-Publication Data
A catalogue record for this book is available from the British Library

1 85856 340 0

Cover image by Fiona Passantino

Designed and typeset by Trentham Print Design Ltd., Chester and printed in Great Britain by Cromwell Press Ltd., Wiltshire.

Contents

Introduction

Barry van Driel

The idea of a book on Islamophobia to bring together some of the leading scholars and educators on this topic from around the globe arose from incidents and developments I witnessed in the Netherlands over the last few years. They made me fear that Western societies are alienating their Islamic citizens and creating an atmosphere that can only lead to further distrust and hostility.

Countries like the Netherlands, Germany, Belgium and France have large and growing numbers of Islamic youth attending primary and secondary schools in some of the larger urban areas. For instance, in Rotterdam, 50 per cent of the population has a recent immigrant background and half of this group is Islamic. The situation is similar in Amsterdam, where the families of 60 per cent of school-aged youth have a recent immigration history. Since these youth will play a critical role in the future, it is important that their voices are heard and that they are not excluded and marginalised. So we should all be concerned about the developments which led to this book.

- In early 2003 Dutch Politician Pim Fortuyn rose to national fame. After his death his fame became international. He created great controversy by stating in a major Dutch daily (*Volkskrant*) that anybody who believed in Islam was '*achterlijk*'. This word fits somewhere between 'backward' and 'retarded' in English. He also commented that the Dutch should only accept non-Islamic immigrants, and turn away Islamic immigrants at the border. The right wing party he led (*Leefbaar Nederland* – Liveable Holland) had him removed from the party for his comments. So he started his own (*List Pim Fortuyn*). Contrary to what many believed, he was able to pull most of the *Leefbaar Nederland* members with him and he attracted large numbers of new supporters. His party grew quickly in the polls and after his assassination became the second largest in the Netherlands. This was a shock for civil libertarians who had always promoted the Netherlands as the quintessential progressive society.

• In April 2003 I was watching 25 high school students at the Anne Frank House, where I work, debating how to balance the right to freedom of speech against the freedom to be protected against discrimination. The debate shifted to whether the Neo-Nazi party NPD should be banned in Germany because of its overt racial propaganda. One girl talked about statements by Pim Fortuyn, who had just been murdered, to make a case that that some of the things the NPD was saying were justified and that it was time the majority spoke its mind and identified the threat that Islam represented to society. Three of the group were visibly Muslim (of Turkish or Moroccan descent). I watched in dismay as they slumped back in their chairs and averted their eyes while this conversation went on. A few other students vocally supported the Dutch girl who invoked Pim Fortuyn's political rhetoric. Most students remained silent, however – bystanders. None came to the defence of their Muslim classmates. Neither the teacher nor my colleague intervened in any way. Given the huge support Pim Fortuyn received from opinion makers throughout society, it is not surprising that the girl felt justified to express her dislike for Muslims. The potential consequences for the hundreds of thousands of Muslim school students across this country of 16 million are part of what this book is about.

• Also in Amsterdam, the city was plastered with two posters in 2002 and 2003 that were extremely insulting to the Muslim youth I talked with. One was an advertisement for a new Middle Eastern restaurant in the city. On the left was a woman dressed in a burka, with only her eyes showing. On the right side was an image of a blindfolded woman of dark complexion, totally nude. The other poster showed an image of a Muslim woman wearing a *hijab* and the text asked: 'how can we liberate them?' This poster was a government public service announcement. The text of the second poster infers that Muslims are strangers in Dutch society – note the word 'them'. It also invokes the symbolic ghost of the 'white man's burden' to bring civilisation to the rest of the world. Neither poster provoked much criticism.

• Various articles had been appearing in the Dutch and other European press relating to the 'hijab issue'. When talking with a small group of Muslim young women they made it clear to me that they had once worn the hijab out of habit, but that it had now become a political statement of solidarity, and made a statement to a hostile outside world. The wearing of hijab has become the focal point of anti-Islamic actions throughout the non-Muslim world. In the United States, an 11-year-old girl, Nashala Hearn, was suspended from school for over a week in the autumn of 2003 for wearing it. This case is still pending, since the parents have filed a lawsuit against the school district. As this book goes to press, the US Justice Department filed a motion in support of the Hearns, stating that: 'No student should be forced to choose between following her faith and enjoying the benefits of a public education'. More than in the United States, however, the hijab has become the symbolic target for Islamophobic sentiment in Western Europe. French prohibition on the wearing of hijab has gained greatest international attention, but the issue is being hotly contested across Europe, as this book shows.

In my conversations with Muslim youth, I witnessed general disillusionment with society due to such reactions. They felt that the majority population, including their school peers and teachers, did not respect who they were. I could clearly sense a growing alienation among these young people.

I became interested in what was happening in the educational world to combat Islamophobia. After visiting several educational conferences, including two of the American Educational Research Association (AERA), probably the largest research-oriented educational conference in the world, I saw that this phenomenon was a blind spot in educational research. Of the hundreds of presentations at the conferences in 2002 and 2003 (and now in 2004), none directly addressed this topic. I hope this book will encourage research on this urgent issue.

The term *Islamophobia* is used broadly in this book. Though strictly speaking 'phobia' refers to 'a lasting abnormal fear or great dislike of something' (Oxford English Dictionary, 1994) we use the term to refer to an irrational distrust, fear or rejection of the Muslim religion and those who are (perceived as) Muslims.

The current societal mood in the West places Islam under a cloud of suspicion and promotes stereotypes regarding Muslims. Contributors in this book refer to this disturbing trend in different countries. Such negative attitudes and resulting discrimination are rarely based on actual exposure to Islam or its adherents. In fact, the great majority of Western citizens have never consciously interacted with somebody Muslim and if they had, would likely not have been aware that the person was Muslim. This same large majority has also never bothered to inform itself about this major world religion or the teachings of the Qur'an. For this reason, the popular media, politicians and other agenda setters can have a disproportionate influence on public opinion.

This book brings together experts from academia and the non-profit world to reflect on the general and specific nature of Islamophobia in Western society, but especially to discuss possible ways of confronting this phenomenon. It is clear from their contributions that Islamophobia is in some ways connected to intolerant attitudes towards minority groups in general, bearing a strong relationship to its cousin Xenophobia. It is also clear, though, that certain aspects of Islamophobia are specific. The solutions proposed in this book reflect this. All the authors, however, underscore the importance of anti-bias programmes in schools.

Tackling stereotypes, prejudice and discrimination in school settings and encouraging an approach that celebrates diversity will not always provide the safe learning environment that traditional Muslim families need. Many progressive and modern approaches to education can be insulting and disrespectful of the culture of Islam. Hermans, who has conducted extensive research among Moroccan families in the Netherlands and Belgium (in press) identifies succinctly but accurately the tensions that can exist between traditional Muslim families and modern Western educational institutions:

> Many Moroccan parents said that schools and teachers did not endorse those aspects of education that they considered important, such as respect, discipline and morality. According to them, although children may acquire knowledge and skills at school, they do not receive a moral education. Schools gave children too much freedom, did not value religion and did not sufficiently recognise the authority of parents. Moreover, children were encouraged to have their own opinions and to question everything too much, even the certainties they were taught at home...

> In many other respects parents said that their religious values and traditions were not respected. Schools forbade girls to wear headscarves, did not respect Muslim holidays, did not always respect religious dietary laws, and gave sexual education that was contrary to Islamic principles...

> Similar feelings were voiced in relation to Moroccan culture. Parents felt that their culture was being disparaged at school. Their children received the message that their culture was backward, primitive and problematic. Morocco was always portrayed as an underdeveloped country and Moroccan traditions and customs were presented as old-fashioned. Moroccan youngsters were portrayed as academically hopeless and in danger of becoming drug addicts or criminals. Women and children were represented as the victims of a harsh patriarchal and traditional culture. It was high time that Moroccans gave up their quaint customs and started to integrate into modern Western society...

> Because of such experiences, some Moroccan parents became convinced that schools had a hidden agenda. They said that in the name of integration, their children were under pressure to dis-

tance themselves from their original culture and to loosen the links with their parents.

These disconcerting research results point to some of the many challenges ahead for the mostly secular public educational systems of Western societies. We can deduce from Herman's study that religious families from various traditions (including fundamentalist Christian families, orthodox Jewish families, traditional Chinese families, etc, feel uncomfortable sending their children to modern secular schools. This has led to the growth of religiously-inspired private schools throughout the West, and with it has come increased segregation.

For many Muslim parents, sending their children to Islamic schools is a preferred solution to removing them from what they consider to be immoral, decadent, selfish, and individualistic influences associated with Western schools. Whether this is a step towards confronting Islamophobia, however, is debatable. Separating Muslim children might allow them to receive the education their parents desire, but it prevents them from exposure to other ideas, values and perspectives. Furthermore, it makes it more difficult for children to acquire the skills to function successfully in a multicultural society, where the majority has a different world-view. If one of our goals is to confront stereotypes, then separation and lack of exposure to others will not help matters.

Another challenge for secular education systems is to define how the word 'secular' is interpreted and what its practical implications should be. Secularism can be defined in such a way that it implies the banning of all talk of religion and belief systems in schools. This is the interpretation given in France, for instance. Secularism can also be interpreted as protecting the religious beliefs of all communities *without favour* and exposing students to the many belief systems represented in classrooms today. This approach has been adopted in the UK educational system, though biases have not disappeared. For many children – and their parents – religion has a major impact on their world view. It shapes their attitudes towards worldly affairs, helps determine what is deemed unacceptable, immoral and taboo, and provides them with meaning in life. When confronting Islamophobia or any other form of religious intolerance, it is difficult to do so successfully when ignoring a key part of one's identity.

The contributions in this book, taken together, show that the phenomenon of Islamophobia has deep historical roots and that the problem is multi-faceted. They also show that it is not only Muslim students who suffer, but that if this phenomenon is not tackled we can *all* potentially become victims of the consequences of Islamophobia. On a positive note, though the authors point to the complexities of the challenge ahead of us, they clearly identify a good number of concrete steps that can be taken in everyday school practice. The many suggestions put forward can significantly alter educational environments to make them more respectful of Islam, its history, Islamic culture and Muslim students. The end result will be a broader view of the world in which we live but – more especially – a safer learning environment for all students.

I would like to end by thanking the many people who supported the publication of this book. All the authors were willing to have their important work edited for clarity and reduced in length to fit the format. It was difficult to cut into texts that contained so much vital information. I especially thank Judy Ford and my wife Fiona Passantino for their suggestions on how to make the book accessible to a larger audience and their editing of various chapters. Fiona, a writer, designer and creator of children's literature, also designed the appealing and striking cover of the book. She helped with the book in numerous ways. If it were not for Gillian Klein this book would have never happened. It was a conversation with Gillian that made it clear to both of us that this book, and more like it, needed to happen. And her editing skills have greatly improved the quality of the book.

1

Islamophobia in North America: confronting the menace

Amber Haque

Introduction

This chapter introduces the reader to the Muslims of America: their population, socioeconomic status, geographical distribution and belief systems. It briefly discusses the concept of Islamic fundamentalism, jihad, the roots of Islam and tensions with the West. The possible causes and sources of anti-Muslim and anti-Islamic sentiment over the last couple of decades is also examined. Short and long-term consequences of Islamophobia within and outside of the educational domain are discussed, together with roles of Muslims and non-Muslims in confronting Islamophobia in the interests of multicultural harmony and common well-being.

In psychology, the term 'phobia' refers to an unfounded or irrational fear. Thus Islamophobia would, psychologically speaking, refer to an unfounded fear of Islam and its followers. The term Islamophobia is relatively new and is perhaps similar in concept to the term antisemitism that describes the hostility Jewish communities have faced. While we may not agree that such vocabularies are always appropriate, they are needed to address and

1

confront existing public attitudes towards a certain minority. The term Islamophobia gained currency due to contemporary political theories espoused by Fukuyama and Huntington and their analyses by political pundits from the West. Fukuyama argued that the downfall of the socialist bloc was good news because it was proof that Western political structures have universal appeal and would prevail internationally. Huntington, on the other hand, paints an ominous picture in which a 'clash of civilisations' will come to dominate the global political scene. Huntington warns against the Confucian-Islam connection and believes that any pre-emptive Western move would be defensive. In his view it is the other civilisations that are stumbling blocks in maintaining a new world order, and they are responsible for creating scenarios that may not suit Western interests. The new world order established after the collapse of the Soviet Union and the first Gulf War is supposedly an order that upholds the interests of the world community as seen by the United States. Huntington's self-fulfilling prophecy proved ominous, as many Western authors, journalists, and politicians started searching for the differences between civilisations, especially Islam and the West. The German Chancellor Helmut Kohl, for instance, made the following statement during a defence convention in Germany in 1994 (Tamimi, http://www.ii-pt.com/web/papers/incriminating.htm):

> The Islamic movements of North Africa have become a source of increasing concern for Bonn and Paris and are being carefully monitored. Security plans for Europe and the Mediterranean basin need careful attention in light of what is happening in Algeria, Morocco, Tunis and Egypt.

Other European politicians have made negative remarks about Muslims and Islam as well. For example, Pierre Lelouche, former key adviser to Jacques Chirac, wrote about the dangers of Islamic fundamentalism in his book *Le Nouveau Monde* and European parliament member Joseph Michele stated:

> We run the risk of becoming like the Roman people, invaded by barbarian peoples such as the Arabs, Moroccans, Yugoslavs and Turks. (Keane, 1993)

Many Jewish-American writers including Daniel Pipes, Steve Emerson, Judith Miller, Bernard Lewis and Martin Kramer have consistently written about the Islamic threat, thereby encouraging the US administration to act against numerous Islamic groups within and outside North America. The recent tough stance taken by the US government regarding the so-called 'axis of evil' and their supporters or sympathisers has compounded the already existing fear and hatred of the US public towards Muslims. Even Islamic belief systems and practices are to some extent perceived as a threat to the lifestyle of Westerners. Across the Atlantic, in the UK, a report by the Runnymede Trust (1997) outlines how 'closed' views – rather than open – in non-Muslim communities have fostered Islamophobia. Islam is now generally perceived as having the following features:

- a monolithic and static religion, unresponsive to new realities

- a religion that does not have values in common with other religions

- a religion inferior to the West; archaic, barbaric, irrational, etc.

- a religion of violence and aggression that supports terrorism

- a political ideology used for political or military advantage

Muslim criticisms of the West are rejected out of hand. Hostility to or dislike of Islam is used to justify discriminatory practices towards Muslims and anti-Muslim hostility is accepted as natural and normal. While unfounded prejudice and hostility characterise closed views, legitimate disagreement and criticism coupled with appreciation and respect typify open views. Thus, Gordon Conway, Chairman of the Runnymede Commission writes about Islamophobia in Britain and the West in 1997:

> If you doubt whether Islamophobia exists, I suggest you spend a week reading, as I have done, a range of national and local papers. If you look for articles which refer to Muslims or to Islam you will find prejudiced and antagonistic comments, mostly subtle but sometimes blatant and crude. Where the media lead, many will follow. British (and American) Muslims suffer discrimination in their education and in workplace. Acts of harassment and violence against Muslims are common.

Islamophobia exists today as a social phenomenon that seems to be omnipresent. It is not surprising that such views, so prevalent in general society, also influence how students view Islam and their Muslim peers. Pejorative attitudes affect classroom interactions between teachers and students and among students.

Both within and outside the educational system, Islamophobia in America has become acceptable – if not respectable. Many Americans who knew nothing about Muslims or Islam are now asking: who are the Muslims of America and where did they come from? What are their religious beliefs? Is Islam a danger to our society? Is Islam a religion of violence? Since the topic of Islamophobia is much too broad to be covered in one paper, the primary aim of this chapter is to increase awareness of the current problem and suggest ways of tackling Islamophobia.

Muslims in the United States

Although the first Muslims may have arrived in the Americas as early as 1178, when Chinese Muslim sailors landed on the West coast (DawaNet, 2003), history books first record Muslims arriving in 1312, when Mansa Abu Bakr travelled from Mali to South America (Nyang, 1999). Of the estimated 10 million African slaves that came to the US in later centuries, around 30 per cent were Muslims. In the 18th century, Moors, who had been forced to leave Spain centuries earlier, were reported living in the Carolinas and Florida. It is believed that most of these early migrants were uneducated and because of forced conversions to Christianity, they assimilated into the mainstream American culture (Nyang, 1999; Shamma, 1999).

Muslim migration to the US in the 19th and 20th centuries occurred in several waves. The first came from the Arab world between 1875 and 1912 and consisted of unskilled people who left the Middle East mainly for economic reasons. Various other waves, which still continue, brought immigrants from numerous nations with large Islamic populations (Haddad, 1991). A development that still has ramifications in the US was the creation in 1930 of the Nation of Islam, headed by Wallace Ford and succeeded by his disciple Elijah Muhammad. These organisations did not preach the teachings of mainstream Sunni Islam and were soon challenged from within by prominent figures such as Malcolm X and Warith Deen, Mohammad Elijah's son. These influential personalities abandoned the Nation of Islam and, together with their followers, joined the mainstream Muslims of America that follow the teachings of the Qur'an, the Muslim holy book and *Sunnah*, the traditions of the Prophet Muhammad. Conversion of non-Muslims took place not only among African-Americans but also those of Anglo-Saxon origin and Native Americans, who embraced Islam for a variety of reasons (Lang, 1997). The name of Muhammad Alexander Russell Webb, a white American and one of the pioneers of Islamic *dawah* efforts at the end of 19th century is familiar to many American Muslims. White American intellectuals converting to Islam were largely attracted by the growing Sufi orders in the US.

Presently, the estimated population of Muslim Americans in the United States ranges from 3 to 6 million. This population is concentrated mostly in urban areas of the East and West coast, the Midwest and parts of the South, especially Texas and Florida (Haddad, 1991; Hussain, 1996). Recent poll data show that 22 per cent of Muslims are US born, 78 per cent are immigrants, 27 per cent are of Middle East origin, 25 per cent are from South Asia, 24 per cent are African-Americans and the rest are from Europe, the Far East and elsewhere (Zogby International, http://www.zogby.com/index.cfm).

Another survey sponsored by Georgetown University in 2001, focusing on urban Muslims, shows that half of American Muslims earn more than $50,000 a year and 58 per cent are college graduates. Seven in ten Muslims are active in their mosques; 35 per cent of men and 26 per cent of women attend religious and/or community services weekly. The poll also shows that 40 per cent of US Muslims are Democrats, 23 per cent are Republicans and 28 per cent are independents. Other findings have shown that 84 per cent want tougher laws to prevent terrorism, 79 per cent support stronger gun control laws, 68 per cent favour the death penalty for murder, and 92 per cent want stricter environmental laws (Project MAPS, 2001).

Islam, Islamic Fundamentalism, *Jihad* and the roots of the conflict with the West

Though it goes beyond the scope of this book to detail political issues such as the present conflict between the West and Islamic nations, it is important to provide some background to the topic of this book – confronting Islamophobia.

Islam has four basic tenets: doctrines, rituals, ethics and legislation. The faith and belief in Allah and His creations and His qualities and His sole worthiness for worship are part of Islamic doctrine. Rituals include daily prayers, fasting, almsgiving and pilgrimage and carry certain benefits for practicing Muslims. Ethics relates to man's intentions as well as external acts that are oriented towards seeking God's pleasure. Ethics, involving high moral character is meant for self, family members and others, Muslims or non-Muslims. Legislation is a set of laws that governs the life of the individual and the community in an Islamic society. Islamic legislation cannot be implemented in a non-Muslim society. Islam asks its adherents to live by the rules of the local government.

In North America, the term 'Islamic Fundamentalism' was coined in 1990 by Bernard Lewis in his Jefferson lecture and published as an article entitled 'The Roots of Muslim Rage' in *Atlantic Monthly*. Thanks to Lewis's stature as an expert on Middle East issues, this lead article and the term Islamic Fundamentalism gained much popularity in the 1990s and strongly affected the West's perception of Muslims and Islam. However, the term 'fundamentalism' is itself alien to Islam and has been used by both religious experts and lay people to refer primarily to those Protestant Christians who believe in the literal interpretation of the Bible, including its doctrines, prophecies and moral laws. If the same term is applied to Muslims, it would refer to those Muslims who also interpret the Qu'ran literally or word for word. The most respected scholars of the Qu'ran caution that literal interpretation can be erroneous, since each event in history needs to be interpreted in its context. The Qu'ran is full of allegories and metaphors and exhorts people to interpret narratives in their proper contexts and extrapolate their relevance to the present socio-cultural situation (10:36), while the final meaning of some verses is known only by God

Himself (3:7). Many Muslims read the Qu'ran naively, without any basic theological knowledge, and extract sentences or passages that suit their personal needs. This is also true for the many non-Muslims who may read the Qu'ran with an inherent bias.

A term that has become synonymous with Islamic fundamentalism is *jihad*. This term is misunderstood by many Muslims and non-Muslims alike. *Jihad* is not 'holy war' (a term synonymous with crusades in Christianity), as the popular media for instance would have us believe, but a struggle in the most comprehensive sense – one that begins with the self and is for the self – to control one's own selfish wishes and desires. Although the Qu'ran does permit Muslims to defend themselves against aggression (22:39), it prohibits them from being aggressors (2:190). While the terms *jihad* and fundamentalism may also be applied to followers of other religions, it is unfortunate that today they are applied only to Muslims.

Tension between Islam and Christianity has existed for over a millennium. The rapid growth of Islam as a religion and creed became a major threat to the Christian West early in Islam's history. Following Muhammad's death in 632, Islam established itself in many Christian lands including Syria, Palestine, Egypt, Armenia, Cyprus and even Spain. From that time onwards, Islam came to be viewed as the religion of fire and sword. What constituted a threat to the West in earlier times is still viewed by many as the case today – theological, political, and cultural differences get in the way of the 'civilised' Christian-West.

Another source of conflict arises from differing worldviews. The current Western worldview is based on the philosophy of secularism, materialism, and scientism. The word 'secular' is derived from the Latin root word *saeculum*, meaning the present age. Thus, secular connotes this world or contemporary times. Secularisation refers to rescuing humanity from the world beyond or turning away from religious and metaphysical control. Although the concept of a omnipotent God is not rejected outright, the secular West largely privatises religious affairs. It is up to individuals to determine how they experience their faith. The kind of present day secularism that has engulfed Western society is based on seeking material happiness in this life. Individual rights, independence and competition are true Western values that are not subscribed to in the same way in other societies.

Islam as a belief system is diametrically opposed to such a materialistic, individualistic and secular worldview. It is based on the ideology of collectivism, interdependence, and a clear set of rules for the individual and society on which there can be no compromise. Islamic values, since they are experienced as being of divine origin, dictate all aspects of a Muslim's life. Islam mandates religious teachings as part of the whole social fabric, including children's education. Since human beings are the creation of God and are sent to earth with a purpose and set rules, they have no choice but to follow God's laws. Freedom is granted to humans as a test and those who use their freedom to reject God's laws are accountable on the Day of Judgment, a notion that runs parallel to Judeo-Christian worldviews. Muslims, Christians and Jews who want to develop a society based on religious constructs thus have a shared agenda.

The similarities between Islam and Christianity as religious belief systems have also become a major problem, since both religions claim their truthfulness in revelation and prophecy. What Christianity claimed about Judaism, Islam has claimed about Christianity – both have declared that their books are final and an improvement over the previous faith's. Mass conversions of Christians to Islam in the past, for instance in the Mediterranean region, also presented a direct threat to Christianity and its power. From the time of the crusades followers of Islam and the West have drifted apart dramatically. The reality is that the latter half of the 20th century transformed Western culture into a world culture. But there has also been a revival of Islam since the middle of the 20th century. Islam is now making its presence felt in the West more than in the East.

Islamophobic trends and their consequences

Since the demise of the Soviet Union and the end of the cold war, the West has focused on Islam as its prime threat. Islamic nations have been attacked, both in the media and militarily. Attacks have also taken place on US soil – anti-Muslim incidents in the US alone rose by over 15 per cent in 2002 compared with 2001 (CAIR Report, 2003). In addition to direct acts of discrimination and violence, the report by the Council of American Islam Relations has analysed the negative impact of post-9/11 government polices on the civil liberties of American Muslims. The USA Patriot Act is one example of a law that *de facto* discriminates against Muslims in almost every sphere of life. Raids on Muslim families and businesses in a number of US states, the Special Registration programme for Muslim visa-holders, and the 'voluntary' interviews conducted with thousands of Iraqi-Americans are examples of continual harassment for Muslims. There has also been increasing Islamophobic rhetoric by prominent evangelical leaders such as Franklin Graham, Jerry Falwell and Pat Robertson. Along with religious and ethnic profiling, workplace discrimination is one area where complaints are common. Dr. Mohammad Nimer, the author of the CAIR report (2003) writes,

> More than any other year, the daily experiences of Muslims in schools, the workplace, airports, and in encounters with the courts, police and other government agencies included incidents in which they were singled out because of actual or perceived religious and ethnic identity.

Such treatment of Muslims obviously has short and long term consequences in the religious, social/psychological, political, economic and educational realms.

Firstly, Islam has been demonised as a religion and its adherents considered backward and violent. This perception makes practicing Islam difficult in Western nations. Muslim places of worship have been attacked in the US, Muslims and occasionally non-Muslims have been killed for their Muslim appearance, Muslim women face ongoing harassment for wearing headscarves and are discriminated against at work, and Islamic preaching has become more difficult. Such attitudes help maintain negative stereotypes about Muslims and prevent non-Muslims from appreciating and benefiting from Islam's cultural and intellectual heritage.

Secondly, Islamophobia creates polarisation in the wider society and provokes discrimination and injustice towards Muslims in all walks of life. Women and children are especially exposed to hostile treatment, making them feel unsafe. Hostility does nothing to foster self-esteem. The young generation born and raised in the West may face an identity crisis and opt to bond more closely with their parents' backgrounds and distrust the West. Such distrust may lead some young Muslims to drop out of mainstream society and this fosters the conditions that make them readily influenced by extremist groups, which offer vulnerable youth a strong sense of identity and purpose. At the national level, such social disintegration can weaken the social fabric of a country when a part of its (educated) minority withdraws from society and fails to contribute effectively to the growth of society at large.

Thirdly, in the area of politics, polarisation is evident between the West and the Muslim world. International relations have soured due to aggressive US foreign policy applied under the guise of fighting terrorism. Religious discriminatory rhetoric has been blatant, even among those in powerful positions. While I was writing this chapter, a high ranking US army general made hateful remarks about Muslims and Islam, calling Allah (God) an idol and stating that Islam was Idol worship. He was defended by the American administration after these insulting remarks. One wonders whether such remarks about Christians or Jews would be tolerated by the American public or media. Amidst all the hue and cry about human rights, it appears that the rights of Muslim citizens is something the majority is willing to sacrifice in its war against a vaguely defined enemy.

Fourthly, on the economic front, Muslim jobs and businesses are seriously affected because of Islamophobia. Talent is also lost to the community at large. Islamophobia has driven some Muslims to return to their country of origin, causing a brain drain from the US. Oil rich countries have reduced investment in the US and talented young Muslims are moving elsewhere for higher education, so US universities are losing out financially. Continued tension in the Middle East has led to enormous waste of money and oil resources, affecting almost all the nations of the world.

Lastly – and this is the overall focus of this book – there have also been consequences for the education of younger Muslims. Muslim girls have been sent home from schools for wearing headscarves. Fortunately, many parents and the Muslim community at large have fought back and this issue is now pretty much under control. But many Muslim students feel a general sense of alienation and exclusion, especially since they are such a tiny minority in almost every educational setting. This is especially devastating for Muslims who were born and raised in the US. They feel rejected in their own country. After 9/11, there was a general reluctance to admit Muslim students of Middle Eastern origin to aviation related programmes. Such attitudes might also have affected Muslims from other than Arabic backgrounds and in disciplines other than aviation or biochemical fields. The Campus Watch Programme instituted on university campuses throughout America presents another major problem. This widespread and influential group has targeted Muslims and their supporters, and has sought to terrorise them through legal means. Although this programme was initiated by certain interest groups, what is disheartening is the involvement and cooperation of the US administration with such organisations, and the shaping of US policies based on recommendations from such groups.

For their own protection, Muslim students have a history of creating safe zones for themselves in higher education. The more educated immigrant Muslims who came from different parts of the globe from the 1940s through the 1960s were especially concerned about the religious and cultural values of their children so they set up the Muslim Students Association (MSA) in 1972 on university campuses throughout North America.

Confronting the menace

What then should be done about Islamophobia generally and educational settings in particular? Both Muslims and non-Muslims have a role to play here. Let me briefly explore, as a Muslim myself, how Muslims can learn to help themselves. First of all, Muslims have a responsibility to gain a better understanding of true Islam. This will empower them to counter attacks on their religious beliefs and also the distortions and false interpretations of Islam embraced by others. An understanding of Islam should come primarily from the two basic sources, the Qu'ran and *Sunnah* – the sayings of the prophet. Having studied Islam first hand, Muslims can view Islam in its totality and at the same time feel confident about their identity as Muslims. It is important they comprehend the intellectual tradition in Islam as opposed to the legalistic approach prevalent in most Muslim societies. While the former addresses the 'why' question, the latter emphasises 'how' and prescribes a list of do's and don'ts without a proper understanding or explanation of the reasons underlying Islamic rulings.

Muslims need to know their history, legacy and heritage and the vast contributions their ancestors made to the arts and sciences. They need to gain a sense of pride in the many accomplishments their religious peers in the past have been responsible for. Muslims should study Christianity and Judaism as well, and understand how governments in the West and in Muslim countries function. This can help them comprehend why Muslim governments have been unable to make independent decisions or install true democracies in their countries. Muslims should engage in an intellectual confrontation with the West and excel in school and at work, thus proving themselves to be contributing members of society.

Since Muslims are a minority in the West, seeking cooperation with other religious communities may also help in attaining certain common goals. There are many Christians and Jews who are willing and able to help Muslims in times of crisis. Muslims in the US could work together with Jews to learn how this community has coped with and overcome antisemitic attitudes over the years. The hard work and positive attributes of the Jewish community, also a small minority, should be appreciated. Muslims must work with people of other religions through interfaith dialogue to extend the basic message of Islam and unite with fellow Muslims to speak with one voice. Muslims may be dutiful when it comes to their obligations towards God (*Huququllah*) in observing the rituals of Islam, but in my opinion they are lacking in their obligations towards their fellow human beings (*Huququlibad*). The latter is evidenced by infighting and violations of human rights, broken families, lack of educational provision and poverty in many Muslim countries. Following all such obligations is also worship if it is done to please God. This would include respecting the rights of other religions.

The followers of other religions lived happily at the time of the prophet and in the prophet's own town of Medina. This was true for most Muslim countries where people of other faiths lived as minorities. The Qu'ran affirms that there is no compulsion in religion (2: 256), so Muslims must strive towards improving their own behaviour and image first, rather than worrying about that of others. The prophet said that a model Muslim is the one from whose tongue and hands other persons are safe. Islam is a religion of peace and that is the way it should be practiced. Some of the misconceptions of Islam in the West can only be confronted in this way.

Muslims' active participation on the US socio-political scene has become all the more urgent after the 9/11 attacks on the US. In my view, it is partially the ghetto mentality of many Muslims that provokes the label of backward. Although Muslims can mix with non-Muslims, this does not mean they have to follow the undesirable ways of others. CAIR's (2003) Community Safety Kit for Muslims offers practical suggestions about how to deal with anti-Muslim sentiment, especially in the area of media relations and law-enforcements.

The majority population in the West is non-Muslim and they have a major responsibility for confronting the growing menace of Islamophobia. I recommend the following approaches and actions for consideration by the larger community:

1. *Education through the media:* The media that is responsible for fanning anti-Muslim sentiment in the West should be used instead to mitigate feelings of Islamophobia among the general public. Independent media agencies that are not biased may be used for this purpose. Debates and seminars on Islam that include Muslim scholars should be aired together with documentaries on US Muslims and their positive contributions to American society. Spokespersons for Islam in the media should be respected Muslims, not controversial figures from either the Muslim or non-Muslim community. More Muslim journalists should be employed by TV and print media agencies. Above all, the media should be reminded of its responsibilities to be pro-social, not divisive. The media

must stop using terms such as Islamic extremism, fundamentalism and terrorism unless they consistently apply them to other religious groups also. Muslim media should be established to air its views in English.

2. *Think tanks*: Committees comprised of scholars from various disciplines and ethnic backgrounds should be formed to identify and confront Islamophobia and the agencies/persons responsible for creating and or promoting Islamophobia. The task of this committee would be to generate government recommendations that influence national policies on intolerance and discrimination against Muslims. This committee could recommend to the government ways of dealing with Muslim communities nationally and abroad, thereby affecting American domestic and foreign policies towards Muslim countries.

3. *Legislative changes and law enforcement*: Islam should be recognised as a major religion in America and its followers protected by law for their religious beliefs and practices. Muslim holidays such as *Eid ul-Fitr*, the first day that follows the holy month of *Ramadhan* celebrated throughout the Muslim world, must be recognised by the government and by US employers. At the workplace, accommodation needs to be made for Muslim religious requirements including clothing, food, and prayer five times daily. Law enforcement officers need to be reminded to observe cultural and religious differences and deal equally with all violators of the law. Cultural sensitivity training about various Muslim practices and those of other minority groups is a crucial part of ongoing professional training.

4. *Special government agencies*: Special agencies should be set up by the government to work solely on promoting racial harmony and resolving complaints relating to a person's racial, religious, and/or ethnic background. Muslims should be included as members of such committees, including a special task force committee to address the problem of Islamophobia. Intensified research is urgently required on Islamophobia and the growing problems faced by Muslim communities in the US. Such research could be spearheaded by social scientists,

whose objective findings would help to define the specialised social and psychological programmes that need to be set up for this minority group. Human Rights and humanitarian organisations should step up their work with Muslims who have been targeted. Non profit organisations can assist in conducting interviews, research and other activities to help the Muslim community and can play a key role in educating the public about the stereotypes that exist about Muslims and Islam and develop new ways to eradicate them.

The educational domain

Two main issues need addressing at the university level: the school/university curriculum and campus problems. Humanities textbooks often carry implicit anti-Islamic messages. These materials need to be identified and removed from college and school teaching curricula, once and for all. This can be difficult, since opposition from certain interest groups is inevitable. However, this can be accomplished with the cooperation of the wider academic community, as well as educational boards and publishers. Small committees can be formed at local level to address this issue and must include Muslim members.

A faculty-student body should be established on each university campus to monitor Islamophobia in pursuit of racial, ethnic and religious harmony. Coordination and communication with appropriate government authorities should be maintained to formulate policies to eliminate Islamophobia. Universities and schools must be made hate free zones by educating students about the true nature of Islam, teaching tolerance and by bringing to justice everyone including Muslims, who violate the law and disrupt the social order and harmony.

Muslim advisors should be hired in schools and on university campuses to provide support services for Muslim students. Muslim dietary requirements should be respected. Prayer facilities should be available on all campuses for every religion represented and teachers must be considerate of Friday prayer times and the month of fasting. While Title VII of the Civil Rights Act of 1964 does cover some of these aspects it is the implementation of such laws that matters. Setting up support groups among Muslim students will create a sense of belonging, cooperation and brotherhood that can be used constructively to confront Islamophobia and at the same time establish a more positive image of Islam in educational settings.

At elementary, middle and high school levels, the curriculum should include an introduction to a wide range of cultures. A guidebook published by the Council of Islamic Education (2003) on handling issues relating to US Muslim students may be useful. The State and Federal governments should consider taking up this task and support the use of 'unbiased' standardised humanities textbooks in all public schools, as this is where chances of delivering biased information are high.

The humanities, social studies and history are all subject areas that offer opportunities to confront Islamophobia and especially the popular belief that Islam is synonymous with backwardness and that Islam and 'civilisation' are opposite constructs. This is false. Muslims have made significant contributions to the arts and sciences – mathematics and medicine, botany, surgery, optics, ophthalmology, physics, chemistry, psychology and sociology. All these disciplines are enriched by original contributions from early Muslim scholars.

Contributions to Arts and Science

Muslim thinkers and scientists, mostly Arabs, include:

- Muhammad al-Khwarizmi (780-847) was the leading exponent of numerals, including the zero, and one of the founders of algebra. His works were translated in the 12th century into Latin and used until 16th century as the principal mathematics textbook in European universities.

- Jabir al-Hayyan (721-815) was one of the great chemists of medieval times. He authored several hundred works and had significant influence on the development of modern chemistry.

- Zakariyah al-Razi (865-925) was known as one of the greatest physicians of all times and, together with Ibn Sina, left an indelible mark on Western science.

- Ibn-Haitham (965-1039) made lasting contributions in mathematics, physics and optics and corrected many scientific misconceptions related to the functions of the eye.

- Ibn Rushd (1126-1198) from Muslim Spain wrote more than twenty thousand pages, according to some estimates, on philosophy, theology, law, astronomy, medicine and grammar and is known as the most learned commentator on the works of Aristotle.

Other prominent Muslim scientists from the medieval period include Ibn Firnas, attributed with constructing the first flying machine, al-Kindi, an authority in geometrical and physiological optics, mathematics and astronomy, al-Biruni, who discovered that light travels faster than sound, developed a theory of rotation of the earth on its axis, accurately determined longitudes and latitudes and introduced Indian chess for the first time, al-Baitar, a celebrated botanist and pharmacist, al-Tusi, who wrote about the size and distances of the planets and planetary tables and how celestial bodies influence things on earth, historiographer al-Tabari, Ibn Khaldun, the father of sociology and modern historiography, Umar Khayyam, the poet and mathematician who reformed the Indian calendar and Ibn Batuta, the renowned traveller who reached Timbuktu, Peking and the Volga (Ahmed, 1967, Nasr, 1983, Muslim Scientists and Scholars, 1998, Hoffman, 2000, MuslimHeritage.com, 2004).

In the Islamic tradition, most if not all these early scholars were more than merely scientists. They were known as wise men (*hakeem*) and possessed knowledge in multiple areas, including religion. The small selection mentioned here are universal figures who left a permanent imprint on Islamic science and made original and lasting contributions to humanity. Sadly, few if any modern-day school textbooks feature these pioneering scientist-scholars. This is due mainly to the biased curriculum developed over the last century, shaped by the colonial masters from the West (see e.g., Sirozi, 2004). In order to repair the damage from such negative practices, school and educational authorities that are serious about confronting Islamophobia need to ensure that children are made aware of these critical contributions to our shared culture.

Conclusion

Although the conflict between Islam and the West is not new, the term Islamophobia is a recent one. The threat of communism has been replaced with the threat of Islam. This threat is relatively new on the North American continent, where the number of Muslims has been increasing steadily. Due to rising Islamophobia, Muslims are now suffering open discrimination and prejudice in all public domains and in education. Muslim students at all levels run the risk of being alienated and turning their backs on mainstream society. If we as a society are serious about combating Islamophobia, US Muslims, the US intelligentsia and the Government must take immediate proactive steps to promote a balanced and accurate view of Islam. Muslims must learn to work with the system in order to survive in the West, while non-Muslims need to show greater respect for a major world religion and its adherents and appreciate what six million American Muslims have to offer US society. Only through such cooperation can a thriving multi-cultural US community be envisioned in the future.

2

Curriculum, ethos and leadership: confronting Islamophobia in UK education

Robin Richardson

During the war in Iraq in 2003 a student at a secondary school in central England approached one of the staff. She was of Pakistani heritage, as was the member of staff. She was being teased, she told the teacher, by other students in the playground and on journeys to and from school. 'We killed hundreds of your lot yesterday ... Saddam's your dad, you love him, don't you ... we're getting our revenge for what you Pakis did to us on 11 September...' The teacher asked if she had told her form tutor. Yes, she had told her tutor, and her tutor had said: 'Never mind, it's not serious. It'll soon pass. You'll have to expect a bit of teasing at a time like this.'

The story illustrates several different facets of the task of confronting Islamophobia within the education system. There is the need, most obviously and immediately, to give support and assistance to young people who are being targeted and attacked. Almost as immediately, students who engage in verbal abuse and banter, or in even worse and more hurtful behaviour, have to be challenged and stopped. Third, there is a range of skills, understandings and qualities required by teachers, and issues around the kinds of in-service training and professional development that should be provided. Fourth, there are issues to do with school ethos; the content of the curriculum; the procedures for dealing with unacceptable behaviour; and school leadership. This chapter considers principally the fourth of these clusters of topics. At the risk of over-simplification and of sloganising, the fourth cluster can be said to be about confronting institutional Islamophobia, as distinct from confronting the attitudes and behaviour of individual students and teachers.[1]

My opening story evokes the complexities of everyday life in a school – the tensions between students, between students and teachers – and between teachers, and the inexorable impact on these of events in the wider world, both in the present and in the past. Often, teachers have insufficient knowledge and understanding to be totally confident that they are doing the right thing; even when they can be reasonably confident, they are painfully aware of competing demands on their energy, attentiveness and sense of priorities, and it's as if they seldom or never have sufficient time and space to think and reflect. Before the chapter gets under way, it is fitting to evoke the complexities of school life with a handful of further stories similar to the one above – stories that are not only about the need for immediate and mid-term action but also about the need for thought and reflection in ambiguous and con-flictual contexts.

Here, for example, is a story which presents the point of view of a young perpetrator. The perspective sketched in the story may or may not be typical. Its portrayal does, however, underscore the need for sensitivity amongst staff, and the need for staff to be clear, both in their minds and in their actions, about what it is exactly that they need and wish to confront:

> A Year 9 pupil was complaining to me bitterly earlier today. 'All right, I'm overweight and I'm not proud of it. But it really gets to me when other kids go on about it. Last week I lost it. I was out of order, right, but when these two kids said I was fatter than a Tele-tubby and twice as stupid I swore at them and used the word Paki, and mini Bin Laden. I got done for racism and was excluded for a

day and my parents were informed and all, and I'm really pissed off, and nothing at all has happened to the kids who wound me up. It's not fair.'

It is not only to behaviour amongst children and young people that staff have to respond and to display leadership. There is also the behaviour and outlook of adults, as illustrated in the next two stories:

> As a secondary school governor I proposed, following discussions with pupils and parents, that there should be some Islamic Awareness classes at the school on a voluntary basis. 'We'd just be letting Al Qaida in by the back door,' said the chair. The other governors all seemed to agree, or anyway not to bother.

> I'm the parent of children aged 4 and 6. They have been desperately distressed by TV footage from Iraq. I spoke to their class teachers. Both said much the same: 'Yes, a lot of the children seem quite upset. But they'll soon get over it. They don't really understand, you know. Don't worry.'

Last, a story from an all-white primary school in rural England. It poignantly illustrates ignorance but also human distress and raises questions about the sources of young children's assumptions and understandings, and the responsibilities of adults, including the media and parents as well as school, in helping to shape them:

> The other day during morning break a boy came running into my office, crying his eyes out. 'The Pakis are coming, the Pakis are coming' he sobbed. I sat him down and calmed him and got him to explain. Apparently, two aeroplanes had flown low over the playground and he had believed they were piloted by terrorists on their way to attack the school.

It is appropriate now to step back from the immediacies of everyday life and to consider wider policy issues. 'There is nothing so practical,' says an old adage, 'as a good theory.' The purpose of the discussion that follows is to clarify theoretical issues such that real, practical life – of the kind evoked in the stories above – is easier to handle. The discussion focuses on cross-curricular review and development; teaching about Islamophobia; support for (British) Muslim identity; explicit policy; and school leadership.

Cross-curricular review and development

The Stephen Lawrence Inquiry report recommended that curricula throughout the UK should be amended with a view to their being 'aimed at valuing cultural diversity and preventing racism'.[2] The respective governmental authorities accepted the recommendation in broad principle but did not tackle it with vigour or with rigour. The three greatest needs in the present context are for:

- an overall framework of concepts and big ideas that should be taught, as appropriate, across all subjects and at all age levels

- guidance on teaching about racism and Islamophobia

- guidance on teaching about Islam

With regard to the first of these needs, one interesting and potentially valuable approach involves identifying themes that should permeate all teaching. One such list is summarised below.[3]

Shared humanity: issues of similarity, sameness and universality
All human beings, at all times in history and in all places in the world, have in common certain basic values, aspirations and needs – there is a shared humanity. Appreciating this is a crucial aspect of valuing diversity and is a necessary foundation for teaching about Islam and Islamophobia, as indeed about many other topics.

Difference and diversity: contrasting stories and ways of doing things
Through history and across the world, there are many different ways of pursuing the same values and needs, and there are different points of view of the same event, based on different experiences and stories. Comparing and contrasting different ways of doing things, and different ways of seeing, viewing and interpreting, is a fundamental human activity. It's important to help pupils see diversity and difference as interesting and exciting, and indeed as valuable, rather than merely confusing and depressing.

Interdependence: borrowing, mingling and mutual influence
Countries, cultures and communities are not cut off from each other. On the contrary, there has been much borrowing, mingling and mutual influence over the centuries between different countries and cultural traditions. Events and trends in one place in the

Mary Seacole Library

http://library.bcu.ac.uk

Renewals: Tel: 0121 331 5278

Borrowing

Due Date

Confronting Islamoph   03/12/2013 23:59
33130469

Racism   17/12/2013 23:59
30675359

19.11.2013 15:57:34

Please retain your receipt

Please check your account regularly

modern world are frequently affected by events and trends elsewhere. A recurring danger in teaching and learning about cultures is that pupils will get the idea that each culture is distinct from all others. The reality is that boundaries between cultures are porous and frequently unclear. Islam and 'the West' are not separate from each other but have developed, and continue to develop, in relation to each other.

Excellence everywhere

Excellence is to be found in all cultures, societies and traditions, not in only 'the West'. The 'default position' in the curriculum, however, can all too often be the assumption that all significant human achievements arose in the so-called West – this is what is communicated, even though teachers do not consciously intend it. The default position has the consequence of marginalising pupils who identify through their families with cultures and communities outside the West, and of miseducating everyone else.

In 2004 an influential UK journalist caused an uproar in British Muslim communities when he polemically illustrated the default position with these words:

> Indeed, apart from oil – which was discovered, is produced and is paid for by the West – what do they [i.e. Arab countries] contribute? Can you think of anything? Anything really useful? Anything really valuable? Something we really need, could not do without? No, nor can I... We're told that the Arabs loathe us. Really? For liberating the Iraqis? For providing them with science, medicine, technology and all the other benefits of the West? ... They should go down on their knees and thank God for the munificence of the United States (Kilroy-Silk, 2004).

Personal and cultural identity

Every individual belongs to a range of different groups, and therefore has a range of different loyalties. Also, and partly in consequence, all individuals change and develop. Pupils need to know and feel confident in their own identity but also to be open to change and development, and to be able to engage positively with other identities.

Virtually all the pupils currently in British schools will spend the rest of their lives in Britain. It is important that they feel they belong here and that Britain belongs to them. In this sense Britishness should be an important part, though not the only part, of their identity. All pupils need to be comfortable with hyphenated terms such as Black-British, British-Muslim, English-British, and so on.

Concepts of race, racism and racial justice
Already at Key Stage 1, pupils need to appreciate that there is a single race, the human race, but that the world is full of ignorance, prejudice, discrimination and injustice. In the course of their time at school they should become familiar with theories about the sources and forms of racism; strategies, actions and campaigns to prevent and address racism, locally, nationally and internationally; equal opportunities in employment and the provision of services; the role of legislation; conflict, and the management and resolution of conflict; intercultural communication and relationships; and justice and fairness.

The framework of key themes sketched above needs to be presented to pupils and students not only directly, as part of the explicit content of the curriculum, but also implicitly and incidentally. This should take place in:

- the exemplars, materials and cultural reference points that are used to illustrate abstract ideas

- the texts, activities, materials and assignments that appear in skill-based subjects, for example ICT, design and technology, literacy and numeracy

- the stories, subjects and situations explored in art, dance, drama and music

- displays, exhibitions, signs and visual materials in classrooms and public areas

- the use of visiting speakers, artists, musicians and storytellers

- assemblies and collective worship

- journeys and visits to places of interest; involvement in national projects

- links with schools in other countries or other parts of Britain; and – not least –

- casual comments and conversations.

Within this framework teachers need to be clear about the nature of Islamophobia and how to distinguish between 'phobic' views of Islam and legitimate criticism. To this topic the chapter now turns.

Teaching about Islamophobia

'Can we no longer even argue with a Muslim?' asked a headline in a British newspaper (Hitchens, 2002). The article beneath the headline was about someone who had been charged with 'religiously aggravated threatening behaviour' following an altercation with his Muslim neighbour. The columnist robustly criticised the police and political correctness – 'the constabulary is terrified of being accused of institutional racism and would probably charge a brick wall with harassment if a Muslim drove into it' – and also the new legislation under which the man was charged.

The journalist went on to criticise the Crown Prosecution Service (CPS), the Human Rights Act and the prime minister's wife and complained about the alleged policing of people's minds and thoughts:

> This is a new crime invented in the mad, hysterical weeks after the Twin Towers outrage... During this period most politicians simply took leave of their senses, which is presumably why the enemies of free speech in the Home Office chose this opportunity to slip it past them. As for the CPS, this incident proves that it's not just dim and useless but nasty as well ... The CPS, which cannot defend the public against crime, is fully signed up to the anti-British, intolerant speech codes of Comrade Cherie Blair and her friends ...The authorities are far more effective at policing ideas than at suppressing crime. Perhaps the CPS should in future have a new name. How about Thought Police?

The headline – 'Can we no longer argue with a Muslim?' – was rather lost sight of as the article proceeded. It was a useful way, however, of posing an extremely important set of issues. Is it really the case that criticising Islam is not acceptable and may even be unlawful? Does action against Islamophobia involve being uncritical towards Islam? How can criticisms of certain aspects of Islam avoid feeding Islamophobia? Is the only alternative to Islamophobia a kind of uncritical admiration?

Shortly after 9/11 another journalist in Britain drew an interesting and potentially valuable distinction between what she called 'mindless Islamophobia' and 'mindless Islamophilia' (Burchill, 2001). She appeared, however, to opine that the latter is considerably more prevalent and serious than the former and directed virtually all her polemic at fellow journalists who try to counter Islamophobia by presenting positive images of Islam in their work. She mocked the BBC for giving airspace to what she called a strong Muslim woman (SMW for short), and for systematically implying that 'British Empire = bad' whereas 'Islamic Empire = good'. There was no mention during the BBC's recent Islam Week, she complained, of 'the women tortured, the Christian converts executed, the apostates hounded, the slaves in Sudan being sold into torment right now'. She continued: 'Call me a filthy racist – go on, you know you want to – but we have reason to be suspicious of Islam and treat it differently from the other major religions ... While the history of the other religions is one of moving forward out of oppressive darkness and into tolerance, Islam is doing it the other way round.'

The journalist's emotive generalisations and imagery ('oppressive darkness') were deeply offensive to most or all British Muslims. Her claim that she was being rational, however, ('we have reason...') was interesting and definitely worth attending to. For clearly there is such a thing as legitimate criticism and suspicion of religious beliefs and practices. In castigating both mindless Islamophobia and mindless Islamophilia she was commending a stance that is mindful. Such a stance is suspicious when suspicion is warranted. But also it is ready, as appropriate, to respect and appreciate.

In a report published in 1997, the Commission on British Muslims and Islamophobia grappled with the problems of debate, dialogue and disagreement. When and how is it legitimate for non-Muslims to disagree with Muslims? How can you tell the difference between legitimate disagreement on the one hand and phobic dread and hatred on the other? The commission suggested that an essential distinction needs to be made between what it called closed views of Islam on the one hand and open views on the other. 'Phobic' hostility towards Islam is the recurring characteristic of closed views. Legitimate disagreement and criticism, as also appreciation and respect, are aspects of open views. In summary form, the distinctions between closed and open views are to do with:

- whether Islam is seen as monolithic, static and authoritarian, or as diverse and dynamic with substantial internal debates

- whether Islam is seen as totally 'other', separate from the so-called West, or as both similar and interdependent, sharing a common humanity and a common space

- whether Islam is seen as inferior, backward and primitive compared with the so-called West, or as different but equal

- whether Islam is seen as an aggressive enemy to be feared, opposed and defeated, or as a cooperative partner with whom to work on shared problems, locally, nationally and internationally

- whether Muslims are seen as manipulative, devious and self-righteous in their religious beliefs, or as sincere and genuine

- whether Muslim criticisms of the so-called West are rejected out of hand or whether they are considered and debated

- whether double standards are applied in descriptions and criticisms of Islam and the so-called West, or whether criticisms are even-handed

- whether no account is taken of the fact that Muslims have far less access to the media than non-Muslims, and are therefore at a competitive disadvantage on an uneven playing-field, or whether unequal freedom of expression is recognised

- whether anti-Muslim comments, stereotypes and discourse are seen as natural and 'common sense', or as problematic and to be challenged.

The words *open* and *closed* were derived from the title of a classic work on the psychology of dogmatism by Milton Rokeach, first published in 1960. Rokeach was primarily interested not in the content of bigoted people's minds but in how their minds worked.

Open-minded people are ready to change their views both of others and of themselves in the light of new facts and evidence, and are fair-minded in the sense that they do not caricature or over-generalise, and do not claim greater certainty than is warranted. Open-mindedness and fair-mindedness are components of what is sometimes termed civility, or moderation, or the middle way. 'At the heart of the concept of the middle way,' writes a Muslim scholar, 'is the principle of fairness, the 'fair play' so integral to the English conception of good character.' He continues:

> Let us be clear about the origin of the English word 'fair', because it shows ... how closely this idea is connected to Islamic principles. The English word 'fair' has two meanings: the first is 'just, equitable, reasonable', and the second is 'beautiful'. But the meaning of the original Germanic root is 'fitting', that which is the right size, in the correct ratio or proportion. The range of meanings of this word 'fair' reflects a truly Islamic concept, the idea that be just is to 'do what is beautiful' (ihsan), to act in accordance with our original nature (*fitra*), which God has shaped in just proportions (Qur'an 82:7) as a fitting reflection of divine order and harmony. (Henzell-Thomas, 2002)

'The core issue,' writes someone whose principal area of academic concern is sectarianism in Scotland, 'is whether minds are closed – viewing other religions (or all religions) as being alien harmful monoliths, or whether they are open – to the facts of diversity, in which religious communities are given respect as people who are sincere in belief, morality and desire to become full partners in political and civic enterprise.' She goes on to stress that it is not only individuals who have closed or open minds but also groups and communities:

> Within every world religious community, whether Christian, Jewish or Muslim, the open and the closed views are in contention. The open communities seek alliance and partnership; extremists of the closed tendency form cliques, factions and sects that can resort to militant action. The 'closed' extremists terrorise their co-religionists along with all the others who stand in their way. (Kelly, 2004)

The distinction between open and closed minds corresponds to the distinction which a Muslim anthropologist draws between inclusivism and exclusivism. In the first instance he is referring to two different ways in which Muslims themselves understand and practise their religion, and relate to others. But his distinctions also apply to 'the West'. He writes:

> Exclusivists create boundaries and believe in hierarchies; inclusivists are those who are prepared to accommodate, to interact with others, and even listen to them and be influenced by them. Inclusivists are those who believe that human civilisation is essentially one, however much we are separated by religion, culture or language.

> ...I believe the real battle in the 21st century will be between the inclusivists and the exclusivists. (Ahmed, 2003)

These admittedly abstract distinctions between closed and open, or between exclusive and inclusive, are of fundamental importance in curriculum planning for all pupils, both Muslim and non-Muslim. With regard to the formation of Muslim identity, and of the views of themselves and others that young British people develop, there is further discussion below.

Young British Muslims

'...There are platoons of young Muslims roaming the streets,' remarked a Muslim journalist in September 2001. 'They saw the TV images of the intifada and copied them during the Oldham riots. Now they are seeing bin Laden turned by the BBC and others into a glamourous Rambo figure. Next time, will they be copying the bombers? We have to invest in forging a positive identity for them so we create the right kind of Muslim' (Nahdi, 2003).

This is a succinct summary of a key educational task – the forging of 'the right kind of Muslim' – and also of the broad international context, interpreted through and by images on television, in which the formation of identity now takes place. Elsewhere the same journalist has warned that a key factor producing the wrong kind of Muslim, as the term might be, is Islamophobia in society, schools and the media:

The war is reshaping our society, and particularly British Islam. For most Muslims it has dramatically exposed how partisan the Western media is – and, for many, how crass Western politicians are and how gullible the Western public is. However, it is the despair, the frustration and the anger that should be noted. Today, Britain's 1.6 million Muslims are living on a diet of death, hypocrisy and neglect that is traumatising and radicalising an entire generation. (Nahdi, 2003)

He writes also:

The combined forces of racial discrimination and Islamophobia have been awesome in the marginalisation and alienation of the community. As a result few, particularly young people, feel they have any viable stake in society ... Our scriptures counsel endless patience. Were it not for Islam, the anti-Western rhetoric and violence would be out of control. Yet, some of us have been tipped over the edge ... (Nahdi, 2003)

British Muslim observers do not, it is important to stress, blame Islamophobia alone for the emergence in Britain of 'the wrong kind of Muslim'. They point also to failures of leadership within British Islam, both intellectual and political. An implication is that the mainstream education system needs to be proactive in making and maintaining contact with mosques and madrasahs, and with the influences within them to save and turn round young Muslims before, by the age of 14 or so, it is too late.

In so far as both the mainstream education system and mosque-centred education fail to reduce alienation and disaffection amongst young British Muslims there will be a vicious spiral of increasing hostility to Islam amongst non-Muslims and increasing rage and resistance towards mainstream society on the part of young Muslims. The time to act is now, not some time in the future. A key role will be played by headteachers and other school leaders.

Leadership

It is mandatory in the UK that all public institutions, including schools and local education authorities, should have a formal, explicit policy on race equality. Also all schools and local authorities are required by law to maintain records of racist incidents. Unfortunately, however, there is no legal requirement that these policies and records should refer to religion. Individual schools and local authorities may use their initiative to make good these omissions. One of the first tasks of leadership, therefore, is to go beyond the letter of the law and to implement also the spirit.

A distinction is sometimes made between 'transactional' leadership and 'transformational'. The Commission on the Future of Multi-Ethnic Britain pointed out that the distinction is particularly relevant to issues of equality and diversity:

> There must be efficient management ('transactional leadership') concerned with the setting of goals and objectives, and holding staff accountable for achieving them. Such management can be summarised in terms of abilities that can be imparted through training courses and assessed with reasonable accuracy.
>
> 'Transformational leadership' is concerned with personal qualities rather than abilities. These include empathy, openness to criticism, a degree of judicious risk-taking, enthusiasm, an aptitude for articulating a vision of how the organisation could be different and better, and a readiness to challenge and shape the opinions of others rather than pander to them. (Parekh Report, 2000)

In a context of overload and uncertainty, of competing proposals, demands and expectations, and of vast geopolitical anxiety, transformational leadership keeps its head and its heart. One of the tasks is to encourage and enable colleagues to wrestle with issues of moment and meaning – not by providing answers but by enabling them to cope with controversy and complexity; not by a finished product but by a focused process. It involves knowing, amongst other things, what's worth fighting for.[4] This chapter draws to an end with a list of the qualities required of all teachers and school leaders in the context of confronting Islamophobia at the present time. With these qualities, understandings and commitments staff will instinctively know what to say and do in the kinds of problematic situation with which the chapter began:

Empathy
Empathy with young (British) Muslim people, the pressures on them from a range of different directions, their determination, their spirit; and empathy with their parents and communities

Listening

Listening to British Muslim children and young people, and being alert to their wishes, aspirations and anxieties, and to how they and their communities are changing

Fairness

Holding the line and the balance between competing demands and pressures; taking a principled stand on the importance of fair play and process

Procedural neutrality

Ensuring that different points of view get a fair hearing, but also that all are questioned, reviewed and discussed

Teachers as researchers

Teachers need time and space to reflect on their own practice, as individuals, teams and whole staffs, and to devise their own ways of improving it

Critical understanding

Critical understanding of religion and religions, and of religion as part both of the problem and of the solution

Muddling through

Accepting that the best can be the enemy of the good, that there is seldom enough knowledge or evidence before action has to be taken, that uncertainty is frequently the name of the game, or much of the game

The culture of the school

Giving focused thought and attention to how your whole school, and also individual parts of it, can embody in daily routine and culture the qualities and values listed above

Hope

Carrying on, despite setbacks and opposition, self-critically but with resolution and determination.[5]

Notes

1 The stories at the start of this chapter are all based on real events. In the form that they appear here, they were written for use in in-service training events. They are quoted from a report of the Commission on British Muslims and Islamophobia, *Islamophobia: issues, challenges and action,* Trentham Books 2004.

2 Stephen Lawrence was a young Black British man who was murdered in a racist attack in London in 1993. An inquiry into how the police investigated the murder, led by Sir William Macpherson, concluded that the police's failure to apprehend the killers, as also their failure to treat Stephen's parents and family with appropriate profes-

sionalism, were due to institutional racism in the police service. The report of the Stephen Lawrence Inquiry, also known as the Macpherson report (1999), contained 70 recommendations altogether. Of these, four were addressed to the education system.

3 The list was developed in Derbyshire LEA and published in abbreviated form in a government guidance document issued in May 2004, *Aiming High: understanding the needs of minority ethnic pupils in mainly white schools.*

4 The phrase is from the title and the content of a seminal text on school leadership by Michael Fullan and Andy Hargreaves, *What's Worth Fighting For in Your School*, 1996.

5 This list of qualities is adapted slightly from *The Achievement of British Pakistani Learners: work in progress* by Robin Richardson and Angela Wood, Trentham Books 2004

3

Islamophobia in German Educational Settings: actions and reactions

*Yasemin Karakaşoğlu and
Sigrid Luchtenberg*

Introduction

Islamophobia in Germany tends to be part of general xenophobia, so that people are seldom overtly rejected on account
of their Muslim faith alone. Nevertheless, there are discourses
where Islamophobia can be detected more specifically, as in the
opposition to Turkey becoming a member of the EU, where it is
openly argued that an Islamic country does not fit into 'Christian'
Europe. Although here part of the discourse is a political 'future-
scenario', there is already an Islamic presence in Germany because of the numerous migrants from Turkey and Northern
Africa. This fact plays a role in political discussions on integration,
which have recently developed a new relevance in Germany. In the
educational discourse – in practice as well as in theory – the
Islamic religion of the migrant student population has been a
major issue of reflection and sometimes also of concern, which
may be rooted in and also evoke hostility against Muslims. We
understand Islamophobia as a general negative attitude towards
Muslim people, their religious symbols and practices. Accordingly

we focus on the most prevalent forms of discrimination directed at Muslims in educational settings.

We begin with a brief discussion of Islam and Islamophobia in Germany and then examine areas of tension between Muslims and the majority society in educational settings, where latent Islamophobia can be detected. We examine how growing Islamophobia can be countered in teacher education. We end with a brief account of how our educational findings relate to the German political background.

Islam and Islamophobia in Germany

From a limited presence in the early 1960s, Islam has become the third largest faith in Germany after the two major Christian denominations. It has also increasingly become the subject of fear and resentment in the host society, especially when it comes to women's role in society and the meaning of the headscarf or veil – the hijab (see Blaschke/Sabanovic, 2000, p. 131).

Although the total number of people in Germany with a predominantly Muslim background had grown to 3 million by the year 2002 – that is 3.4 per cent of the total population – the majority society still remained surprisingly ignorant about them and their religion. Only recently has Islam been treated as an issue in schools and several Christian-Islamic circles have been established since the mid-90s. These were initiated to counteract rising xenophobia in the majority society after the reunification of the two German states in the early 1990s. At this time, the largest Muslim community in Germany, migrants of Turkish origin, was the target of several hostile attacks by right-wing groups made up of German youth.

Among the intellectual, spiritual, artistic and practical expressions that constitute the cultural identity of a specific group, religion is of major importance for Muslims in Germany. According to recent surveys in the Turkish community, two thirds of young people consider themselves to be religious or very religious. As far as religious practice is concerned, Turkish migrants – more than those from Italy, Yugoslavia or Greece – practise their religion regularly in everyday life. More than any other manifestation of their cultural values, Islam is regarded as the feature that most strongly differentiates them in terms of identity from the majority host society. In a survey on youth in Germany in 2000, financed by the Shell Foundation, Turkish and German young people found that in everyday life they differed most from each other in their religion, followed by family life (Deutsche Shell, 2000, p 249).

In debates about Muslims in Germany, religion is often viewed as an obstacle to integration. This would appear to be based on a definition of integration that equates it with assimilation. Yet questions of German attitudes to and the integration of Muslims are not just cultural. The official political attitude to migration, both of the government and the population, is of central importance.

The development of Islam in Germany has been influenced by a number of factors (for details see Karakaşoğlu, 1996; Lemmen/ Miehl, 2002). The most important among these are (1) the trend in the migrant community from supposedly transitory migration to permanent settlement, (2) the associated trend from a homogenous male community of workers to a heterogeneous population whose members can be found in all walks of life, (3) socio-economic developments both in the host society and in the migrant community and (4) political developments in Turkey, links between the two states, and international events. In combination, this results in a higher number of migrants practising Islam on a private level and the creation of (mainly Turkish-Islamic) mosque-organisations – partly with a political background, of which only some smaller groups may be labelled 'Islamist'.

Currently, Islam is the best-organised of any of Germany's ethnic and religious minorities and the Islamic organisations are mainly Turkish. Among the others, the Muslim Brotherhood (mainly Egyptian, but also active in other Arab countries) is active among parts of the Arab Muslim population in Germany, while 'Shia' activists are known to be influential among Lebanese, Palestinian and Iranians as are other Shia-related groups, such as the Alawi. In addition, the heterodox Ahmaddiya movement, favoured by some German converts, were significant in the construction of mosques in Hamburg, Frankfurt and elsewhere in West Germany in the 1950s.

Until recently, Turkish mosques were without exception situated in the industrial areas of large cities or attached to housing complexes. This was partly because these communities had scant financial resources to erect new buildings of their own. More important, though, were the reservations of the host society about buildings that looked recognisably 'Islamic'. It was only through struggle that 'real' mosques could be built, that is mosques with domes and minarets, which are very much part of the 'real' mosque image for Turkish Muslims. This is only one example of resistance by the host society to migrant Muslims' pursuit of their constitutionally guaranteed cultural and religious rights. The arguments presented by the host society included (1) the fear that the mosque would become a magnet which could turn the neighbourhood into a ghetto, (2) parking problems, (3) the argument that the architecture of a mosque would not fit into the overall cityscape and (4) the argument that a mosque could foster the spread of Islamic fundamentalism. We consider such arguments to be a form of institutional Islamophobic discrimination.

Furthermore there is the failure to recognise the second generation of Muslims as belonging to German society. Even those born in Germany were, up to January 2000, treated officially as 'foreigners'. For those of Turkish or other non-German origin locally born and bred, the stigma attached to their supposed 'foreignness' still restricts access to the labour market, public life, and political participation. A reaction to this lack of recognition in the host society is to contemplate instead their 'own' values, which they find in Islam and its precepts. The socio-economic situation of the Muslim migrants is also an issue. The unemployment rate of Turks is twice as high as for the overall German population. There is a housing shortage, and educational disadvantage: migrants' children are over-represented in less academic schools and under-represented in the schools for academic 'achievers'. In this hostile context, Islam offers psychological support and reassurance for a credible and secure safeguarding of values. Religion is thus acquiring an increasingly important place not only for its own sake but also in reaction to social problems. This response and Islamophobia are closely connected, with the majority of Muslim migrants constituting a kind of ethno-religious sub-proletariat in Germany.

In addition, there is a growing fear of xenophobic attacks, which have increased along with the host society's economic problems after the reunification of the two German states. The 'different' migrant population is an easily identifiable scapegoat. Ironically, this tends to drive the people targeted further into that very 'difference' i.e. Islam.

Islamophobia after September 11

No official figures are available for the verbal or physical attacks against Muslims in Germany since there is no institution that collects or analyses acts of discrimination and hostility. In the immediate aftermath of the events of September 11, reporting institutions saw 'a rise in Islamophobia and more widespread physical tension' in Germany, but they realised that with time 'such hostilities steadily decreased'. In general, physical attacks are 'quite rare, but the level of verbal abuse increased significantly'. Most often, the targets of these attacks are women wearing a headscarf and men of 'Arabic appearance' (EUMC, 2002b, p19). Many Muslims report that they perceive growing mistrust towards them, expressed in hostile behaviour like 'staring or whispering behind their backs'.

Recent surveys on the attitudes of Germans towards Muslims (Leibold and Kühnel, 2003; von Wilamowitz-Moellendorff, 2003) present a contradictory picture with respect to the nature of Islamophobia in German society. In the study conducted by Leibold and Kühnel (2003) 25 per cent of the respondents said they would refuse to move to a Muslim dominated neighbourhood, 15 per cent feel alienated in their own country because they believe too many Muslims are living here and 10 per cent feel that Muslim culture does not fit into Western society. On the other hand, according to the same broad German representative study, a respectable 30 per cent think that Islam has created an admirable culture. The study points to the high correlation between xenophobic and Islamophobic attitudes. People who are xenophobic are mostly Islamophobic too (Leibold and Kühnel, 2003, pp. 102-107).

In a study conducted by the Konrad-Adenauer-Foundation, 87 per cent of the respondents who have not yet had personal experience in a Muslim neighbourhood would not feel disturbed by having Muslim neighbours. But nearly half of the German respondents in this study consider Islam to be intolerant (von Wilamowitz-Moellendorff, 2003, p. 2). Thus it can generally be stated that, in comparison to other hostile attitudes towards special groups of people, Islamophobia tends not to be a very distinct issue in Germany, even after September 11, but that latent mistrust of Muslims is prevalent, especially in the new states of Germany. This occurs more often among women than men, more among elderly than younger people, more among people in blue-collar jobs and with a lower level of education (von Wilamowitz-Moellendorff, 2003, p. 13).

It has also been reported that, when dealing with the issue of 'Islam', German officials tend to pass the matter on to the department for national security. This was the case in the dragnet investigation looking for sleeper cells of the al-Qaeda organisation in Germany. But this also applies to all the other issues concerning the presence of Islam in public and especially in educational institutions in Germany.

Problems experienced in educational settings with the articulation of Islamic demands

Contrary to what sociologists and educators in the 1980s expected, the significance of religion among the youth of Turkish origin in Germany has not declined. Today, 80 per cent of the Turkish but only 45 per cent of the German population view religion as very important for a satisfying life. Young Muslims born in Germany, especially the well educated, are strongly inclined to develop their own approach to religion that is often quite different from the traditional popular Islam their parents adhered to. We can see a process of rising self-esteem in every field of public life and the desire for access to public space, articulated both individually and collectively. The identification by the majority society of Islam as 'fundamentalism' has long led to such needs being ignored. This accompanied an apparent failure on the part of state institutions to recognise and rate Islam equal to other world religions present in Europe – all this in the context of a growing xenophobic reflex aimed mainly at the Turkish population. The effects of this, which may be understood as latent Islamophobia, can be seen in the following different educational settings.

Teaching Islam in German Schools

The German concept of secularism is not a radically lay one. It has never been effectively severed from society's Christian roots. Freedom of religion, as guaranteed by article 4 of the German constitution, does not only imply the right to believe or not to believe, to practise or not to practise one's faith in public, and to maintain religious institutions and organisations, but that religion may also interfere with individual and communal freedom. The need for the separation of religion and state in Western democracies is often misunderstood to mean the separation of religion and politics, which does not exist in Germany. As a result, the Christian Churches and also the Jewish community have their own official representatives; they are entitled to membership of various social and even political groups. In all German states (*Länder*) church taxes are collected by the state, and in most of them religious education is part of the public schools' regular curriculum. Teachers of religious education need permission by both the state and their Church to practise. No such thing is possible for Muslims in Germany, because the immigrants' religion lacks the hierarchy that characterises the Churches' organisational structures.

Because of this specificity, the issue of teaching Islam in German schools is controversially discussed (see Bauer *et al.*, 2004). While Muslim migrant associations regard themselves as representatives of the majority of Muslims in Germany, German officials point out that only about 20 per cent of Muslims in Germany are members of these organisations so there can be no representation for Muslims analogous to those of the Churches. Since the states are responsible for education, religious education for Muslims in German schools varies, though it is mainly included in mother tongue education (Behr *et al.*, 2003). Since 2000, model projects have been created in some states to test new possibilities for religious education of Muslims in German. While in North-Rhine/ Westphalia and Bavaria these have been conducted by the state, in Berlin and Baden-Württemberg Islamic organisations are involved in their development and realisation. Bremen has recently started to establish religious education for Muslims as a state project without the participation of the Islamic lobby. As the state is not allowed to interfere in or rule the religious affairs of communities, these models lack the authorisation of Muslim representation. The main reason to establish them was to counterbalance the conservative and sometimes separatist orientations of certain Islamic organisations and their Qu'ran courses. Even if this seems understandable, the state nonetheless projects lack a legal basis.

Participation of Muslim students in Physical Education

Using the arguments of European Enlightenment, such as 'human rights', 'freedom of religion', etc., Muslims have begun to pursue religious-political aims. They use such arguments for example to release Turkish girls from the obligatory participation in mixed physical education classes, on the grounds that these are incompatible with their sense of modesty required by religious obligations. A high administrative court in Berlin decided in August 1993 that the right to freedom of religion is more important than girls' statutory obligation to participate in non-segregated physical education. Only if the school is able to segregate the sexes for physical education will Muslim girls be obliged to attend further.

The court's decision is still controversial in schools and cases continue to be reported where girls (or boys) are forced to attend mixed physical education classes (see Blaschke and Sabanovic 2000, 106f.). If they refuse they have to accept low grades for not participating. School representatives justify these measures with their enlightened understanding of physical education: i.e. co-educational physical education is a part of teaching the equality of the sexes in society. Since co-education is now viewed more critically by German educationalists, concepts of 'reflective' co-education, which demand separate education in some subjects, will reconcile Muslim and bureaucratic demands. Another domain causing problems between traditionally oriented Muslim parents and schools is residential school field trips. Some parents distrust the teachers' supervision of overnight stays.

Although the case of being released from attending mixed sex classes in physical education may appear to be a 'conservative' phenomenon, the significance is that it was pursued and won on grounds of European notions of human rights.

Wearing the headscarf: students and teachers

On the grounds of religious freedom, Muslim students are legally protected to wear headscarves in classrooms. Nevertheless, the issue repeatedly provokes emotional debates at schools as to whether it should be permitted. As some German teachers and school directors regard the headscarf as a symbol of back-wardness, oppression of women and of disintegration in the host society, they practice various strategies to reduce the number of headscarves worn at their schools. A protestant secondary school in Gelsenkirchen, for instance, only allows their Muslim girls to wear the hijab after they turn 14 (the official age of religious maturity in Germany) and after being interviewed by a school council regarding their reasons for doing so. In other schools, psychological pressure is put on parents not to 'force' their daughters to wear this sign of disintegration – otherwise they might face problems in school and society.

One young Muslim teacher was at the centre of a controversy about whether Muslim women teachers should be allowed to wear 'Islamic dress' in German schools. Fereshta Ludin, a young woman of Afghan origin, was trained as a teacher in Baden-Württemberg. According to their Ministry of Cultural Affairs, the headscarf was at variance with basic Christian values and constitu-tional secularism alike. As a symbol of backward, fundamentalist Islamic attitudes, it was viewed as opposing the principles of free-dom of thought and of the equality of the sexes. Arguing against this image of the headscarf, Ludin emphasised in interviews that she would always defend those two societal principles, and that it was her own decision to wear it, as a personal symbol of what Islam meant to her. She also stressed that she did not consider it a way of putting Muslim girls under pressure who did not wish to wear a headscarf. While public debate continues, the Federal Con-stitutional Court stressed in a final decision in September 2003 the necessity to treat all religions in Germany equally. If Baden-

Württemberg wants to remove all religious symbols from school, it has to establish a law.

The Ludin case turned out to be a critical case for all the other states in Germany. The discussion gained momentum after the Christian Democratic Party of North-Rhine/Westphalia and Bavaria decided to establish so called 'anti-headscarf laws', which give Christian symbols a privileged position over Islamic or others. The decision of the Federal Constitutional Court was followed by a continuing and heated discussion among politicians, journalists and the wider public focusing on why some young Muslim academics stick to wearing a headscarf, whether they are ruled by extremist organisations and to what extent teachers at state schools should appear 'neutral' in their outward appearance. Seven of the 16 state parliaments are consequently now occupied with preparing an 'anti-headscarf law' or 'law against all religious symbols worn or used by teachers in state schools'.

The Ludin case demonstrates that German state authorities, much like a considerable part of the population, still tend to regard the headscarf in general as evidence of an undemocratic, theocratic and thus dogmatic world view. Teachers with head-scarves are suspected of imposing a backward world view on their pupils and considered a potential threat to democratic and tolerant education.

Empirical evidence proves this assumption to be false. More and more young Muslims want to play an important role in public life in Germany, to have a position in the community, without neglecting their specific approach to Islam (Karakaşoğlu, 2003). It even seems that being visible as a Muslim in a secular non-Muslim environment is not only a matter of personal preference, of life-style, or of searching for individual or collective identity, but perhaps also an important and effective way for members of a minority to be recognised with their special religious demands and their distinct identities, both individually and as a Muslim lobby.

In many cases, symbolic dress serves young Turkish girls as a token of 'externalised' religiosity. It does not always reflect a desire to gain a reputation for personal religiosity in all areas of life. It may also express completely different and quite individual views of what constitutes an Islamic way of life. If one's religious orientation stresses an allegedly Muslim style of clothing, this is still not necessarily related to a conservative and dogmatic world-view. The religious orientation of young students wearing a headscarf is quite different from that of their parents. It is important for them to claim that their way of life complies with the rules of the one and only 'true' Islam, as opposed to traditional Turkish Islam, which they regard as a culturally estranged religious hybrid. The desired outcome is to be able to live in Germany as a believing Muslim who plays an important role in the secular public sphere. The German approach to Islam in the educational field is thus not only a sign of latent Islamophobia but also at risk of rejecting young Muslims as equal citizens.

Teacher training

In most states, university courses on initial teacher training do not include an obligatory unit in multicultural education, though some universities offer seminars on multicultural topics. Religion plays only a marginal role in these courses and seminars and even in an obligatory introduction into multicultural education, religious questions are just one topic among many. Racism, on the other hand, is tackled more often, making it possible for Islamophobia to at least be raised.

Student teachers are often ill informed about the religious situation in Germany, and especially on Islam. This became obvious in one of our recent education seminars. Though the seminar itself was on a different topic, media competence, one session dealt with migration as portrayed in the media. This session was prepared by students and centred on the headscarf discussion in the German media. The attitude towards Islam was surveyed with the help of an anonymous questionnaire, and the responses revealed a lack of knowledge too often replaced by prejudice. Twenty-two graduate students, mostly women student teachers or MA students in Education, took part. Most of them were Christian, predominantly Roman Catholic, and a few declared themselves to be atheists but there were no Muslim students in the group. One of the three students presenting the session wore a headscarf – something she had never done before. Married to a North African

Muslim but not herself a Muslim, she is familiar with the hijab and traditional clothes. Below we summarise some of the results.

Question 1: Please state three associations with Islam.

Qu'ran (11) and mosque (10) were the associations most often given. These answers can be evaluated as neutral since they refer to two main manifestations of Islam, comparable to Christianity's Bible and church. The third association – headscarf (10) – is on a different level since it is not a central component of Islam. But it is not surprising that it was mentioned so often: political as well as private discussions on Islam often feature the headscarf, as in the recent media reports and the political arena concerning women teachers and other professionals. Furthermore, the headscarf is the most visible sign in Germany of Islam, since mosques are often hidden in factory buildings and the like. Some of the other responses were neutral, such as Ramadan, Mecca or Allah, but many associations were negative – such as: oppression, wars, terror, 'jumping on burning flags' or 'hand chopped off'.

Two of the other questions dealt with people's views of the role of women and men in Islam – an area where stereotypes are to be expected because media reports, both fictitious and factual, are full of them. The students expressed the usual stereotypes, reflecting a rather negative view of Muslims. Women were characterised as suppressed (11), living in a traditional role as wife and mother (13), while being subordinate to father or husband (5). Most of the further characterisations were related to this image, and only a few students mentioned emancipated observers of Islam. All answers based their views – often explicitly – on the measure against a model of modern, Western secularised society. The men were seen as being in a dominant position (7), the master in their household (10), who generally assumed leading positions (8), although slight change was presumed to be taking place.

How the media deal with the hijab was the focus of the seminar session. Students worked in groups to analyse different texts from the print media and discussed the issue of school teachers who wore a headscarf. The following questions were asked:

- Is a teacher wearing a headscarf 'neutral'?

- Is it a sign of tolerance and integration?

- Should teachers be allowed to wear a headscarf when teaching?

There were serious discussions and some agreement. A general tendency against the headscarf was obvious:

Against	No preference	Sign of integration
5 (1 split)	1	1 (from the viewpoint of Germany)

The reasons given reveal the poverty of their knowledge about the role of religion in Germany. Some students expressed the opinion that according to the constitution, Christianity is the state religion. They did not understand the secular character of German society. One group was concerned whether 'a teacher with headscarf would be able to teach Christian traditions at Christmas'. Others objected on the grounds that a Christian German teacher would probably be forbidden to wear a cross in Muslim countries.

These results confirm that student teachers know little about Islam so can easily be influenced by the media, which are mostly hostile or at best disapproving towards Islam. Teacher training therefore has a double task: student teachers have to confront both their own prejudices against and rejection of Muslim lifestyles and at the same time learn how to reduce Islamophobia in schools.

The most prominent recommendation to meet these challenges is the promotion of inter-religious encounters. This notion is rooted in the concept of multicultural education, where encountering 'others' plays a dominant role. But neither teacher education nor school teaching offer much space for such meetings, at least not officially. Multicultural education offers some possibilities, and with diverse student groups now attending teacher training courses, it is possible to visit churches, mosques, synagogues and other places of worship. In many universities, religious groups – Muslim, Jewish or Christian – are open to such possibilities. In schools, intercultural encounters often occur in science, history or social sciences, while religious subjects are normally separated –

even in the Christian denominations. However, since Islam is a religion that is far more significant in daily life than is Christianity today, it should be included in intercultural programmes (Lemmen and Mieh, 2002). It might help non-Muslims understand the problems of living a religious life in a secular society (Donohoue Clyne, 1998), and enhance the awareness of differences in life philosophy between a secular population and one for whom religion is part of daily life. Only through insight into these differences can the chances for a common life in a common state and society be revealed.

Many Germans, however, regard a life dominated by religion as a step back into medieval conditions. So those involved in such programmes need to understand the complexity of the task.

Models of conflict management

The aim of intercultural programmes is to focus on mutual understanding and to avoid conflicts, but differences can easily create conflict and conflict has to be managed. In schools, for instance, a Muslim student may refuse to sit next to someone of the opposite sex or participate in sports. Or the teacher might describe a Muslim holiday or fasting during Ramadan as 'strange behaviour'. Parents are often involved in such conflicts because the school calls on them to provide solutions. Or conflict may arise with teachers when parents insist on special treatment for their children. Few teachers in Germany are trained in conflict management other than recently, in combating violence in schools. Even worse, teachers learn little about the school-parent-relationship, and seldom anything about migrant parents or parents with different cultural and religious backgrounds to their own. Instead, the media generate stereotypes, for instance about the suppression of Muslim girls, which easily become part of professional educational opinions, as the seminar results show. Thus, it becomes the parents' fault when a Muslim girl refuses to take swimming lessons.

Aspects from conflict management programmes can be used to train teachers for these unexpected situations. A principle of many such programmes is that the conflict partners have to discuss the issue with the help of a 'neutral' person, a mediator, who may belong to the status group of one of the partners but must put the subject of the conflict in the centre, not the antagonists. This mediator could be another teacher or a representative for the parents.

Multicultural communication concepts can be applied to training teachers where the focus is on the development of mutual empathy and understanding. They can foster competence in looking for compromises, such as single-sex sports classes or food provided on excursions respecting the requirements of Muslims. Meetings that apply such concepts will contribute not only to improved mutual understanding but also to reducing Islamophobia.

Teaching acceptance

Assuming that many teachers may, like other people, succumb to Islamophobia as long as Islam is mainly characterised negatively in the political and media discourse, it is unlikely that they will teach their students to accept religious diversity. This makes educating and training teachers crucial. Other factors may also lead to a reduction of Islamophobia in schools:

- Schools that adopt the philosophy of multicultural education require that education is inclusive (Gundara, 2000). Teachers will have to accept all students as having the same rights, and this includes expressing cultural or religious differences.

- International exchanges, common in German schools, help comprehension of the German situation. The French laicist approach, with its secular pattern and its strict rules with respect to all religions, is not applicable in Germany, whereas the British model may evoke reflection on how much difference is tolerable without major irritations.

- Examples of gaining knowledge about different religions can be integrated into teacher education and training and also help disseminate knowledge in schools. Knowledge is only the first step however. Empathy is the second.

The study of religious and cultural diversity is an essential element in teacher training since teachers can contribute to mutual understanding if they themselves are at ease with diversity. Teachers and student teachers should not be manipulated but should gain insight into multiculturalism by being enabled to encounter different cultures and religions, learn about different philosophies and discuss their impact on German society – and schools. Teachers do not have to accept the rules of Islam but they need to accept the right of Muslims to follow their rules as long as they do not contradict Human Rights or German laws. Teacher education has to prepare German teachers for our multicultural, multiethnic and multi-religious society far more effectively if it is to diminish Islamophobia.

Conclusion

Muslim immigrants and their demands for equal participation in every realm of society have done much to revitalise the debate on the role of religion within the German state. Views about how religion relates to modernity are controversial. The position of Islam in a basically Christian yet secularised society is crucial: will Islam be allowed to achieve a social position similar to that of the Christian Churches? The Churches, with their many social and economic ties with the German state, will not willingly surrender their privileges in favour of a radically laicistic separation of state and religion.

Islamism which represents a form of political extremism should be watched closely and, in its violent form (such as the case of the Kaliphat State Organisation) be banned in Germany. But it is significant that official data from the Federal Office for the Protection of the Constitution shows that Islamists and those propagating extreme ideologies constitute only 1 per cent of Muslims in Germany.

Policy makers still need to develop a code of practice for religious equality that will meet the challenge of religious pluralism which *de facto* already exists. The German President, Johannes Rau, pinpointed this need when he intervened in the current debate on Muslim teachers wearing headscarves, in his New Year's speech in 2004. He demanded that all religious symbols should be banned in schools, opposing the bills aimed at banning only the hijab but not the cross or the Jewish kippa. This drew strong criticism, especially from the President of the Bundestag and representatives of the churches, who see the headscarf as not only a religious but also a political symbol and a mark of the subordination of women.

Equality for Muslims will be a possibility only when they themselves can together address their own interests. But the majority society does not admit them as equal partners in the discussion. Islam and Muslim customs becoming accepted in Germany will depend on whether young Muslim academics will be able to enter key positions in the German democratic system. If they succeed in gaining a share of the power, they might develop and articulate fresh approaches to Islam as an integral instead of alien element of German society.

4

Intercultural Education in Europe: A recent history of dealing with diversity and learning to live together

Pieter Batelaan

Introduction

During the 1970s and 80s, schools in Western Europe absorbed a large influx of immigrants, mainly from the Mediterranean region. Countries such as the UK, France, Germany, Belgium, the Netherlands, and Sweden had started to become immigration countries, although some still find it difficult to acknowledge this. Countries such as Portugal, Spain, Italy, Yugoslavia and Greece were considered and considered themselves to be countries characterised by emigration.

The main concern at that time was to prepare the children of these migrant workers for the existing school system and to make sure they could successfully complete a school career. Important (political) issues related to whether 'foreign children' should be educated in separate classes, the development of second language programmes, the status of the home languages, and the relations between countries of origin and host countries – for instance whether to recruit teachers for 'language and culture of the home countries'. This situation is different now: Southern Europe is in a similar situation to Northwest Europe in the 1970s and 80s. Eastern European nations have recently joined the league of democratic countries, and they have discovered their own ethnic, national or cultural minorities and have become fully aware of their responsibilities towards them.

The events of September 11, 2001 changed the European landscape once again. Though the attacks were on New York and Washington, citizens of many European nations were among the victims and survivors. Vague feelings of discomfort among the majority non-Muslim population readily found an outlet as the world turned to scrutinising Islam. Discomfort became distrust and many sought explanations for the horrific events in something inherent in Islam and followers of this faith. The challenge to values and norms based on equality and tolerance in such a climate is clear.

More generally, policy makers such as the Council of Europe, and professionals working in social institutions such as schools, have become more aware of societal conflicts and controversies that relate to the co-existence of people with diverse value orientations due to the events in 2001. Europeans in the educational realm have become more aware that 'multiculturalism' implies far more than celebrating diversity but also implies dealing with conflicts and dilemmas within the framework of democracy. This is particularly the case where the cultural values of some are at odds with certain democratic standards of equality, for instance with respect to gender. We have become more convinced that living together peacefully, based on mutual respect, is not automatic. It is something that has to be learned, learned by everybody, and the target group is not only students belonging to a minority, but all students. The goal is not only to do justice to diversity and to create equal opportunities but also to learn to live together, even when we have different views of equality, democracy, justice, religious doctrine and behaviour, individual responsibility, what is right and wrong and so on.

We (I speak in this chapter as a non-Muslim to other non-Muslims) may proudly proclaim that most Muslims – or Jews, or

Africans or Catholics – are democratic, and this is no doubt true. But we must also realise that we might have students in our classrooms with different definitions of democracy, or students who feel that democracy is not always the preferred political model. Creating a safe learning environment for all students means creating a safe learning environment for these students as well. After all, various modern Western societies have histories that include episodes of dictatorship and non-democratic decision making.

In spite of myriad local and regional differences, the basic principles of all members of the Council of Europe tend to coincide in:

• doing justice to diversity and providing for each citizen, irrespective of her/his geographical, ethnical, cultural, social or religious, background

• providing equal opportunities to participate in democratic society, including the economic, social, educational and cultural infrastructure

• freedom of thought and opinion.

My introduction has sought to clarify a specific concept of intercultural education that can generate concrete measures that can be taken to address the topic of this book. In my many years of work across Europe, North America and Asia, I have found that there are more similarities than differences when it comes to developing and implementing strategies that deal with issues of tolerance and intolerance at the level of the school and the classroom.

Intercultural education and perspectives on intervention

In order to envision any kind of educational intervention, for instance when confronting Islamophobia, we need to distinguish the various perspectives that parents, classroom teachers, schools, policy makers and the students themselves have. We need to distinguish and respect the different roles that each stakeholder has in the educational process. We need to distinguish between intercultural education as a set of conditions to be fulfilled in order to provide equal opportunities for all students and intercultural education as content (curriculum and organisation of learning processes) to achieve the goal of learning to live together. This chapter focuses on the teacher and the school.

Much has been written about the differences between intercultural education (more common in Europe) and multicultural education (more common in the USA) and the chapter is informed by inter-cultural education, though North American readers may find it useful to equate the term with multicultural education.

To address a phenomenon like Islamophobia, I believe we need a whole system approach that embraces intercultural education at its core. The two main principles of this approach are

- inclusion and participation

- learning to live together

Table 1 reflects the main components of these approaches, based on my years as a teacher, teacher educator and as editor-in-chief of the academic journal *Intercultural Education*.

Table 1: Characteristics of Intercultural Education

Inclusion/participation	Learning to live together
Which implies:	*Which implies:*
Equal opportunity policies	Tolerance/anti-discrimination/anti-racism
Equal access	Human rights education
Language policies	Education for citizenship
Cultural and linguistic rights	Communication and co-operation
Special care for groups/ individuals at risk	A reflective, critical attitude
Validation of specific skills and knowledge	Conflict management
Cultural responsiveness	Dealing with controversial issues
Mainly conditions to be fulfilled by policy makers, and professionals	*Mostly content-related*

Most literature and research on intercultural education pertains to one or more of these implications. The same applies to policies.

In general, European and North American nations still focus primarily on language issues, such as an additional or second language in English-speaking countries, and special measures to assist so-called minority groups. These are important and can assist, for instance, Muslim students in their schooling, especially if they come from an immigrant background. We need to realise, however, that learning the language of the school is only one part of a more complex strategy to integrate minority students into the school system, make them feel safe and comfortable, and motivate them to learn and reach out to others who may have a different religion or set of values. It is also critical that teachers gain further insights into the cultural backgrounds of their students and be culturally responsive, applying these insights, among others, to help them ensure that all students can participate equally in the learning process. We educators also need to take into account the need to learn to live together, particularly when confronting issues of racism and discrimination. It is the *coherence* between these various themes that makes intercultural education effective.

Let us have a closer look at the two main principles.

Inclusion and participation
Democracy is characterised by pluralism – doing justice to diversity – and the provision of equal access. Diversity and inequality are two sides of the same coin. While the challenge for *politicians* is how to ensure that different *groups* in society can participate in and benefit from the existing educational and cultural infrastructure or to adjust that structure to promote inclusion, the challenge for *professionals* – the teachers and school leaders – is how to ensure that *each individual* gains access to the learning process. Each individual is unique. Diversity at the classroom level implies far more than ethnic and/or racial diversity. The challenge for teachers is having to deal with a multitude of diversities they encounter in their classrooms: their students' interests, talents, individual and family histories, physical conditions, social conditions (including legal status), peer status, gender and also their cultural and religious background, ethnicity and race.

All of us tend to overlay our own values, expectations, experiences, identities, stereotypes on the people we meet and the diversity they represent. This helps us cope with the almost infinite number of variables we encounter in our daily interactions. Too often, however, we base our interactions, attitudes, interventions and expectations on one or two – usually visible – identifiers. After September 9/11, being Muslim became one of the key identifiers for many educators, even if the students themselves feel uncomfortable about such categorisation. One can compare this to the way many assimilated Jews in Germany in the 1930s and 1940s who did not identify strongly as Jewish were forced by society to view themselves primarily as such. When teaching individual students in the classroom, one cannot isolate a single category. It oversimplifies a complex reality and closes our minds to other sometimes more salient personality dimensions. So we cannot assume that because somebody is Muslim, or Roma, or Black, or a woman, or Latino, or Asian that their behaviour can be explained by their belonging to this social category.

Equity at the classroom level refers to equal access to the interaction taking place in the classroom. Providing this access and making sure that every student can participate is a major responsibility for every teacher, because participation is the key to success, however defined, for learners. The number of students participating is a quality concern.

Equity requires specific competences which should be a feature of teacher education and further professional development. It requires also that the school provide certain conditions in terms of policy and organisation, as we will see.

Learning to live together

At the level of learning objectives, the main aim of intercultural education is learning to live together. Our societies are diverse in terms of identities, cultures and interests. And that can make it difficult to live peacefully together. Learning to live together is eventually aimed at shared citizenship at the local, the national and the global level. Though we are different, we need to share a feeling of belonging to a wider community, based on mutual respect and a shared belief that dialogue is indispensable. In its broadest context, this means the development of a sense of global citizenship.

Learning to live together should be reflected throughout the curriculum, and this implies that the state too has a responsibility. Although there are major differences between the educational systems of the European and North American nation states, all have subscribed to UN, UNESCO, Council of Europe, and OSCE conventions and recommendations concerning promoting respect and tolerance. Accordingly all these countries have an obligation to promote respect and tolerance. For each of them, dealing with issues of diversity and learning to live together belongs to standards of quality. What does this imply for practice at classroom level, from the teachers' perspective, and at school's organisational level?

The teachers' perspective

Within the classroom environment, the main instruments for teachers are the *content* and the *interactive processes* they have to organise. Content and interaction processes together constitute the curriculum. Table 2 on page 60 lists some characteristics of intercultural education at the classroom level.

People gain understanding through interaction, discussion, and the application of knowledge. The role of the teacher as a facilitator, observer, manager and evaluator of learning processes, not just a provider of information, has been promoted in recent years by educational authorities, researchers, teacher educators, and school managers. The emphasis on interaction in intercultural education is wholly in accord with this new professional identity of teachers. 'Learning to live together' implies learning to learn together, talk together, work together, and to solve problems together through dialogue.

Co-operative learning in which all students participate, and which does justice to the students' different skills and insights, is crucial to achieve the aims of intercultural education in general, and to confronting a climate that allows Islamophobia to rear its ugly head in particular. Co-operative learning in the framework of intercultural education implies a specific strategy in order to ensure that each student participates and that their varied skills, talents and insights are valued equally.

Table 2: Intercultural education at the classroom level

	1. Content	2. Interaction
1. Dealing with Diversity and Providing Equity	The curriculum reflects the reality of multicultural society and presents reality from different perspectives	The teacher makes sure that all students have equal access to the interaction and to the materials
	The curriculum deals with issues of pluralism, which include religious pluralism	The teacher provides opportunities to participate, using the knowledge and skills of each individual student.
2. Learning to live together	The curriculum deals with issues of tolerance, human rights, racism, and discrimination	The teacher provides opportunities for communication and co-operation in heterogeneous groups and for reflection
	The curriculum includes the issue of different and shared values, which are often controversial	
	Communication skills	Mediation strategies
	Conflict management	
Relevant subject areas	History, literature, Language, arts, citizenship education, geography, religion, cross curricular activities	All

Implementing new educational strategies in order to achieve the goals of learning to live together has implications for teachers' professional needs, and therefore for teacher training. Teachers need to know how to

- organise co-operative learning in classrooms in such a way that all students participate and can be held accountable for their contributions

- organise dialogue in such a way that students experience such dialogue is meaningful

- identify and validate the various skills, knowledge and insights that students bring into the classroom

- deal with status issues in the classroom, as these affect participation

- discuss controversial issues from a position of respect for diversity within the framework of human rights principles
- deal with conflicts.

The perspective of the school

Educational policy and research is eventually aimed at school development: at improving quality in terms of relevance, effectiveness and organisation. Improving quality is not the responsibility of individual teachers but primarily of the school as an institution. Improving quality is currently interpreted in many nations as improving test scores, to the exclusion of other measurements of quality. But there is more to education than the three Rs. If we are to create responsible, insightful citizens who can interact successfully in a variety of social and cultural situations, this quality must be viewed and assessed in these terms. We cannot lose sight of the fact that human beings are social beings.

Remaining silent when students are excluded and marginalised because of their religious beliefs, or because of other visible or invisible identifiers is not a viable option, even if ignoring and avoiding problems often seems like the most convenient response. Too often educators close their eyes, hoping that the problems will just disappear. Sometimes they do; sometimes they simmer unseen. Without a school culture that can recognise what is below the surface, we may never know the reality until it is too late. Providing a school culture that can identify problems early on is a quality issue.

Improving quality as we define it here requires clear policies, coherence, a culture of openness, communication, and accountability. In short, it requires good governance and management. Without supportive leadership in the school, efforts to implement programmes to address Islamophobia can become inconsistent or half-hearted. Teachers need to understand that their colleagues and the school leadership will back them up when they encounter the almost inescapable problems that accompany any kind of intervention. This means developing a school culture that promotes diversity and a commitment to confront prejudice and discrimination, and promotes inclusion.

In sum, if we are truly to confront Islamophobia and its equally unpleasant cousins in educational contexts, we will need more than temporary *ad hoc* solutions.

5

The Subtleties of Prejudice: how schools unwittingly facilitate Islamophobia and how to remedy this

J'Lein Liese

To be free is not merely to cast off one's chains, but to live in a way that respects and enhances the freedom of others.
Nelson Mandela

Introduction

Mohammed [all names have been changed], an Iraqi student at an Arizona middle school, was excited about making an Iraqi flag for the school's nations parade during its annual multicultural week. However, in light of the Gulf War, the school's principal 'thought it best' that all Iraqi students walk under the banner of the American flag so the other students would be less likely to discriminate against them.

Whether the principal's actions were discriminatory, well meaning or simply misguided is open to debate. Since the Gulf War in 1991 and especially since the tragic events of September 11, 2001, American schools have struggled over how to balance promoting respect for differences and patriotism, on the one hand, and fighting 'the war on terrorism' on the other. This chapter assesses the complexities surrounding this debate and offers some strategies for educators to prevent Islamophobia from becoming inherent in the school community.

Differentiating people and politics

One major problem with the principal's decision to ban the Iraqi flag from the school's parade is that it sent a message to Iraqi students that they should be ashamed of or align against their country of origin. The US's problem with Iraq was not with its people but with its President's decision to invade Kuwait. Most Iraqi refugees in the United States shared similar sentiments about Saddam Hussein, but that doesn't mean they had to feel shame or anger about their own ethnicity, culture, religion or country of national origin.

Not only was the principal's decision potentially harmful to the young Iraqi students in his school, but his decision also risked promoting anti-Islamic sentiment and prejudice among the overall student and staff population. His decision had the potential consequence of both ostracising students of Middle Eastern descent and creating an atmosphere that might encourage verbal and physical violence on campus. Resiliency research has demonstrated repeatedly that children who feel ostracised at school are at greater risk of joining gangs or engaging in maladaptive behaviour (Garbarino, 1999). The principal lost a wonderful opportunity to promote the difference between politics and people and encourage a positive and inclusive atmosphere of diversity on his school campus. He chose avoidance instead of education, effectively putting his students in danger of long-term ignorance by failing to address the misconceptions, stereotypes and prejudices the students might harbour.

The role of fear and perceptions of threat

Prejudice and discrimination may originate as a personal disposition or orientation in response to a particular social group or its symbolic representation (Esses *et al*, 1994). In post-9/11 America, prejudice toward Muslim and Arab students appears to be derived more from social stereotypes – beliefs shared among members of a community – than personal stereotypes based on actual experience. This is of especial concern because the pejorative stereo-types against Muslim students are often justified, as we have seen, in the guise of patriotism.

This conflict escalation model helps illustrate the impact that 9/11 has had on the psyche of the US population, especially young people.

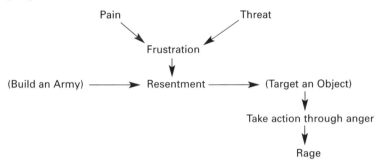

Sixteen years of working with young people in the areas of race relations and violence have shown me repeatedly that students who feel pain or threat, particularly over something out of their direct control, often come to experience frustration and resent-ment towards the social groups they blame for their feelings. This process removes any blame from oneself or one's in-group and places all blame on an outgroup that is perceived as threatening in some way. Yet, perhaps because human beings have a conscience and a 'good' person doesn't simply dislike another person unless he or she feels justified to do so, when young people reach the level of resentment, they tend to *build an army* of support for their negative feelings toward other groups among their peers and even prominent adults in their lives. Once they can acquire agreement from others about the characteristics they attribute to their target, any actions stemming from anger, suspicion or rage can be deemed justified. With American society experiencing both pain and threat in this new age of terror, the target of some American youth's feeling of pain and threat has, sadly, become Arab and Muslim students.

This phenomenon is not new. Since the 1940s, social scientists have been exploring what has been called the scapegoat theory of prejudice (Zawadzki, 1948). The scapegoat theory suggests that when hostilities are aroused through frustration but cannot be directed at its source, because the source is absent, unidentifiable, or too powerful, the hostility will be displaced onto a non-instigating target. And present circumstances are conducive to scapegoating. With communisim no longer a threat, the new enemy of the US is conveyed by the media and other information channels as difficult to identify precisely. It is unpredictable and seemingly omnipresent, yet elusive. This has created a constant state of low-level anxiety among many youth, repeatedly reinforced by government warnings of impending attacks on innocent Americans.

Berkowitz's (1989, 1990) cognitive neo-associationistic model states that negative affect aroused by unpleasant events activates anger-related feelings, thoughts and memories as well as aggressive tendencies. Additionally, Esses, Haddock and Zanna's (1994) mood and information processing model suggests that being in a negative mood state, whether caused by frustration or any other unpleasant occurrence, increases the likelihood of expressing negative stereotypes of other groups.

Thus it is not surprising that in consequence the current 'war on terror', Islamophobia is rising in US schools, as various organisations have documented. The challenge for educators in such a climate is to develop strategies to prevent and dismantle potential negative stereotypes, prejudice and racism. Before considering solutions, let us first examine the different levels of intolerance educators can encounter in school settings.

Levels of prejudice and discrimination
(Adapted from the National Conference for Community and Justice's Anytown Curriculum)

Educators need to be cognisant of the different levels of prejudice and how escalation can happen. The following will illustrate the different levels that commonly occur on school campuses.

Level One: Verbal Slurs
'If they are not terrorists themselves, they are probably related to one!' – 16 year old high school student

The first level of racism prevalent on school campuses is the use of verbal slurs. Often deriving from stereotypes, a slur is often described as a word used to demean another person (http://encarta. msn.com/dictionary_/slur.html). However, in today's society, it could be argued that the purpose of a slur can be to *dehumanise* another person or social group to justify committing a violent act. For instance, rarely do teachers observe young people referring to each other by name before or after a fight. They hear instead things such as '*We beat those punks!*' more often than the racial slurs used to justify violent behaviour. If human conscience does exist, humans would have a difficult time committing violent acts against one another. So they first try to dehumanise their target group. Especially in times of war, most countries have labels dehumanising the enemy because young soldiers might find the trauma of consciously thinking about killing Juan, Muhammed, Sylvia, Vladimir Jr. or their father, son, brother, sister or grandmother too difficult to bear.

In today's 'war on terror', the dehumanising terms *terrorists* and *evil doers* are slurs that have been used to justify retaliatory actions post 9/11 (President Bush's State of the Union Address, 2002). Unfortunately, these slurs have been absorbed into the American psyche and young Muslim and Arab youth are facing the consequences in US schools.

Level Two: Avoidance

'*It's not that I have anything against her, I don't even know her. But I don't feel comfortable talking to her because she seems so different.*' – 16 year old high school student describing why she had not talked with a new Palestinian student who wears a headscarf.

Avoidance is common on school campuses. Usually because they wish to stay within their comfort zones, young people will most likely avoid their peers who have a different appearance or social group membership to their own. We see this in lunchrooms, at breaks and in the journeys to and from school. Often, youth will reinforce stereotypes by using verbal slurs among themselves to strengthen group bonds and to justify their rationale for avoidance, so creating a unifying force to maintain distance from the person or persons to be avoided.

Level Three: Discrimination

'*They were probably just joking around but the boys pulled off my head-scarf when I was walking down the hall. Other kids told them they weren't right to do what they did, but I still felt embarrassed.*' – 17 year old Muslim student

The combination of verbal slurs and avoidance can lead to overt discrimination. In the incident above, a group of boys were laughing and encouraging each other to pull off the girl's head covering. Other students had intervened to help the girl. An investigation by the vice principal revealed that the perpetrators had had no previous social association with the girl but had made her the object of their jokes because she looked different. This eventually led to overt racist behaviour. The principal had a difficult job disciplining the boys because the victim was reluctant to pursue charges. Already embarrassed, she did not want to bring further attention to the situation. Unfortunately, this is a common response by victims, who are already conscious of 'standing out.' Many victims are also fearful that taking action will make things worse.

Counter-measures to support the victims who may want to avoid participating in disciplinary procedures include actively promoting pro-social peer intervention. In this case, the principal could have drawn on the students who condemned the attack to help spread a positive message among the student population. They had taken a stand and were excellent role models. And had this school had a peer mediation programme in place, the victim might have been more inclined to work through the issue with her peers instead of relying solely on adult staff. School-wide anti-bullying policies, subscribed to by both students and teachers can be extremely effective.

Levels Four and Five: Violence/Murder

Prejudice taken to its extreme may result in violence and, in extreme cases, murder. Sadly, racial fights are not uncommon on school campuses. Arguments that have nothing to do with race or ethnicity can turn racial when combatants resort to verbal slurs to express their anger.

So how can social ills such as Islamophobia be addressed in school settings? The answers are not always as clear cut as we would like them to be.

Diversity or adversity: promoting respect amidst a culture of fear

Combating prejudice and discrimination needs to go hand in hand with developing strategies to induce students to respect each other, especially if there is potential for conflict. Addressing the issue of how to approach diversity effectively has been a continuous challenge for US schools. McCaine's (1993) ten per cent rule illustrates a common debate in US schools attempting to address diversity. According to this model (Figure 1), schools taking steps to develop a plan to promote respect and understanding about racial, religious and cultural differences risk creating polarisation.

McCaine demonstrates how ten per cent of educators believe firmly in promoting the concept of 'sameness'. *We are all human or we all have the same colour blood* or *there is only one race, the human race* are the arguments by those who favour this approach. On the other side of the spectrum are the educators who take a stand for exploring differences. *A person's experience of being an American is directly based on the colour of one's skin* is used to promote this viewpoint.

The problem with the ten per centers is that both sides tend to be blind to the other's perspective – when actually a balance of both approaches would be the most helpful in promoting a respectful

Figure 1

McCaine's 10% Rule

10% of school personnel teach sameness	10% of school personnel teach differences

80% of school personnel are
confused
ignorant
tired of the conversation

campus environment. Furthermore, the ten per centers tend to be so strong in their opinions that the 80 per cent in the middle – the greatest mass – often feel unheard or intimidated and/or grow tired of the whole argument.

When we add America's current 'war on terror' and post 9/11 fears into the equation, the promoting sameness approach risks promoting denial and avoidance of the current challenges facing Muslim students. The often-heard phrase after 9/11 that 'We are all Americans' can serve to unite in times of adversity, but also risks ending any conversation about the specific needs and situations of the communities that are disproportionately affected by such events. Crises such as 9/11 are an invitation to learn, listen and communicate and should be accepted.

Dismantling prejudice and racism
Who do we focus on?

Some educators will deny that there are problems in schools because there have been no violent incidents. They are then surprised when incidents occur later. Merton's Typology of Prejudice and Discrimination provides a framework for understanding why negative attitudes, for instance towards Muslim peers, do not always lead to direct discriminatory behaviour, even though negative attitudes are widespread among the student population (Farley, 2000).

According to Merton, there are two types of liberals and two types of bigots:

Figure 2

Merton's Typology on Prejudice and Discrimination

	Does not discriminate	Discriminates
Unprejudiced	all weather liberal	fair weather liberal
Prejudiced	timid bigot	all weather bigot

Source: Farley (2000:56)

The all weather liberal is open in attitude (unprejudiced) and behaviour and likely to remain tolerant irrespective of the situation. All weather liberals would most likely be the students willing to make the first effort to get to know their peers from different cultures. But adolescence can make it difficult for many students who wish to be all weather liberals to act accordingly, since peer pressure and the need to fit in often determine students' behavioural choices. Thus, many students whose value systems promote tolerance and understanding may find themselves more in the fair weather liberal category, where if the social climate is liberal they too will be liberal. These go-with-the-flow students will discriminate if their peers call for it, despite their general open and accepting attitude. One task for schools and educators is to promote a school culture that will support students to engage in activities that promote intergroup understanding and which identify and defuse tensions in the school, such as diversity clubs, discussed later.

On the other side of the spectrum are the bigots – the students who overtly and covertly promote prejudice and discrimination on campuses. According to Merton, there are two types of bigots: the active bigot and the timid bigot. Active bigots are the easiest to identify because their actions are usually overt and demonstrated through both their verbal and active behaviour. Their racist behaviour can be expected and they are are unlikely to try and hide. The timid bigot on the other hand, who has the same discriminatory and racist attitudes as their actively bigoted peers, will not act on their beliefs unless their peers take action first. The key for educators is to prevent timid bigots from acting on their attitudes while at the same time challenging these attitudes. The more their attitudes and behaviour correspond with the attitudes and behaviours of important reference groups such as parents or the others in their gang, the more difficult it is to deal with or shift bigots of either kind.

Strategies for educators to dismantle prejudice and discrimination

This section briefly describes some useful first steps in addressing Islamophobia and related phenomena. I focus on middle and high schools, since Beth Finkelstein deals specifically with younger children in the next chapter.

Let us first examine an incident that took place in my own community, since it illuminates some of the problems that occur when intergroup problems are inappropriately dealt with.

Several years ago at a Phoenix high school, an African American male student allegedly made unwanted physical contact with a white female student. It was never fully determined whether he 'pinched' or 'patted' her bottom. This should have been treated as an incident of sexual harassment, but because the students were of different ethnicities, a racial fight ensued resulting in over 50 police officers intervening, wearing full riot gear, and an emergency dismissal of all students from the school. Rather than creating an opportunity for student dialogue to discuss the issues at hand, the school chose a containment response and kept police on the campus for several days afterwards, until the student population was deemed to be calm once more and life had returned to 'normal.' As with the principal's missed opportunity over the flags, avoidance of discussion and dialogue was the strategy adopted. At the level of attitudes nothing had really been solved. This is hardly surprising when so few teachers believe conflict resolution and the promotion of intergroup harmony to be part of their professional task. Few are trained to deal with issues such as Islamophobia, racism and other forms of intolerance.

However, if school is to be a safe place for all students to learn in, principals, teachers and other stakeholders must work together with students to create a safe learning space for all. Only in such a climate can intolerance be tackled. Based on my experience in various countries, I suggest below some general strategies to create a school atmosphere that can start to tackle intolerance. I also point to some proven effective national programmes that can be used to combat Islamophobia as part of a broader campaign towards intercultural understanding in schools.

General strategies

1) Develop zero tolerance of verbal slurs

Most conflict escalates from verbal abuse by students. Often racial comments directed at an Arab or Muslim student will be disguised as patriotism, so putting the teacher in a challenging situation. However, if a zero tolerance policy on racial slurs is in place, this can help alleviate tension and forestall conflict.

This includes educators taking the stance that directing the word 'terrorist' at someone in the school represents a slur. This may excite controversy, but denouncing terrorism is different than referring to people as terrorists. Terrorist action must be kept separate from an identified group of people, so as to avoid fostering negative stereotypes.

A word on Zero Tolerance...

Many schools implement a policy of zero tolerance by automatic suspension of students. That is not necessarily the best form of implementation, especially if the goal is to educate the students and increase respect and understanding across different ethnic and cultural groups. Zero tolerance should rather entail mandatory opportunities for education, such as peer mediation and/or dialogue groups that allow students to explore their fears and feelings as well as listen to other viewpoints.

2) Promote authentic pride

It is important that young people develop an authentic sense of personal and cultural pride. It could be argued that one cannot truly respect and value others until one values oneself.

However, there is a difference between authentic pride and false pride. False pride takes the form of standing up for who one is personally or culturally by comparing oneself to others and putting down those who are different. When pride is authentic on the other hand, one is comfortable enough with oneself so has no need to compare or compete with others who are different. Since 9/11, there has been a rise in patriotism in America. Patriotism can be an important unifying factor and every young person should feel a sense of authentic pride in their country and culture. However, false patriotism, meaning patriotism that is experienced, for instance, by judging other cultures and countries as wanting when compared with the US, is a potential formula for conflict, both on school campuses and in the community. Anytime a 'better than' debate is promoted, conflict is practically inevitable.

3) Establish a diversity club
Diversity clubs are excellent ways of promoting respect and understanding for cultural differences while providing young people with an opportunity to develop authentic pride. The key to a successful diversity club is an adult advisor who is adept at facilitating young people's ideas and providing the support needed to bring them to fruition. Often it is the school's diversity club that will organise programmes such as the 'Mix It Up at Lunch' day, discussed later in this chapter, or use the school's in-house morning announcement video system throughout the school year to promote understanding and appreciation of the school's diversity.

Club meetings not only provide a chance for students to plan events but also to discuss issues of concern. Successful clubs often divide their meetings into two parts: the first part to give a chance for students to talk through current events and issues they deem important, within a supportive environment where they can safely ask questions and explore fears, thoughts and judgments in a way that promotes understanding of differing viewpoints, and the second part to focus on implementing club projects. Clubs that tend to focus only on projects risk losing members as, typically, the bulk of the tasks tend to fall upon the group leaders. Others can easily feel left out, leading to attrition of membership.

4) Use inclusive methodologies
Cooperative learning methodologies are much more suited for discussing issues of tolerance and intolerance than the lecture format because, if done well, they involve all students in the discussion. For a further discussion of this type of methodology see the preceding chapter by Pieter Batelaan.

A few specific programmes to address stereotypes, prejudice and discrimination
'*We don't have anything against other groups, we are just more comfortable hanging out with each other.*'

This was the answer a group of high school sophomores gave when asked why they only ate lunch with other white students instead of mixing with others on campus.

What might persuade young people who prefer to stay within their comfort zones to initiate friendships with students who are culturally different?

Mix it Up

A first step in moving towards preventing or dismantling stereotypes and prejudice is for schools to create opportunities for students to 'expand their comfort zones' as it applies to the diverse ethnic and cultural groups on any given campus. Although this can be done in a multitude of ways, one successful approach has been the Southern Poverty Law Center's 'Mix It Up at Lunch' programme (www.mixitup.org). In the 'Mix It Up' programme, students take on the challenge of identifying, questioning and crossing social boundaries. The developers of the programme recognised that social boundaries, such as staying within their social comfort zones among peers, can create divisions and misunderstandings in schools and communities.

Although many high school principals and teachers agree in theory that diversity programmes are needed to promote respect and understanding on campuses, these programmes are often seen as time consuming and few staff members feel equipped to facilitate the emotionally charged dynamics that may arise. Accordingly, the Mix It Up programmes has created methods for schools to participate through: Mix It Up at Lunch Day, Mix It Up Dialogue Groups and Mix It Up Grants.

In 2002, more than 200,000 students throughout the United States participated in the first Mix It Up at Lunch Day. They committed to sitting somewhere new in their school cafeterias and with someone new to them. In 2003, more than two million students from 7000 schools across the country participated.

Mix It Up Dialogue Groups are supported by a user friendly handbook for schools to promote authentic dialogue among students. Developed in conjunction with Study Circles, the programme allows students to get to know each other and learn from each other's viewpoints. Mix It Up Grants are special funds that student activists can apply for to initiate projects on their campuses promoting respect and the crossing of social boundaries.

Other national programmes available to schools that can help address racial, ethnic, religious, etc. divisions include:

Anytown – National Conference for Community and Justice
Established in 1950, Anytown is a residential leadership programme for high school students, designed to strengthen cultural
awareness, racial understanding, inter-religious respect and
gender equality. Currently, these programmes take place in 40
cities throughout the United States (www.nccj.org).

A World of Difference – The Anti-Defamation League
'A World of Difference' programmes provide hands-on training to
help students and staff challenge prejudice and discrimination and
learn to live and work successfully in an increasingly diverse world
(www.adl.org). ADL offers curricula for schools, universities and
community based organisations.

Conclusion
Dismantling prejudice, especially Islamophobia, requires vigilance
among educators. Recognising the subtle levels of prejudice and
racism and actively working toward respect and understanding is
not easy.

The US used to be called a melting pot. Today it is more like a
flower garden and it is the different sizes, shapes and colours that
make a garden beautiful. However, every garden has the potential
to grow weeds. If these weeds are not removed, the garden will
lose her beauty. Since 9/11, the US is at risk of developing the
weeds of stereotypes, prejudice and racism and it is its Arab and
Muslim youth who are likely to suffer. The strategies outlined in
this chapter are by no means conclusive, but they seek to offer
educators a few ideas to help pull the weeds, continue to plant
seeds and allow their garden to grow.

6

Practical Educational Programming that Confronts Islamophobia

Beth Finkelstein

Introduction

Despite the significance of religion in public life in the United States, school curricula generally fail to address issues regarding religion and interreligious understanding. This omission, when combined with increasing Islamophobia, renders educational programming to prepare children for our pluralistic society imperative, notwithstanding the complicated and difficult history of religion in public schools.

The Tanenbaum Center for Interreligious Understanding's *Building Blocks for Democracy: Children Celebrate their Traditions* programme has created a unique set of curricula for students in kindergarten through the fourth grade that educates students about different religious traditions and also teaches the skills for living in a pluralistic and democratic society. Unlike other programmes that target older students, Building Blocks is presented to children in their formative years, when they are most impressionable.

This chapter introduces readers to the Tanenbaum Center's educational programming, and describes the rationale and conception for the programme's design, and its implementation.

Religious life and Islamophobia in America

The United States is one of the most religious countries in the Western industrialised world. About 90 per cent of Americans believe in God and 80 per cent of Americans cite religion as an important part of life (Nord and Haynes, 1998). The US is also one of the most religiously diverse countries and immigration, especially from Asia, Africa and South America continues to extend the diversity of American religious life (Eck, 2001).

The Muslim-American population of the US is growing fast. According to the General Social Survey, the Muslim-American population increased from 0.2 per cent of the population in 1973-1980 to 0.3 per cent in 1981-1990 to 0.45 per cent in 1991-2000. Although different researchers report different statistics, some experts report that there are more Muslims in America than Jews or Episcopalians (Eck, 2001).

The US is also witnessing an increase in Islamophobia and anti-Muslim incidents. The third annual poll on religion in American public life, jointly released by the Pew Forum and the Pew Research Center in the summer of 2003 indicates that, '44 per cent of the American public now believes that Islam is more likely than other religions 'to encourage violence among its believers" (Pew Forum, 2003 p1). In March 2002, 25 per cent of Americans indicated they felt this way. A report released in May 2004 by the Council on American-Islamic Relations (CAIR), America's largest Islamic civil liberties organisation, reported that anti-Muslim incidents in the US increased by almost 70 per cent. The annual study records 1019 incidents of violence and verbal abuse, more than CAIR has ever recorded.

All too often, schools are the backdrop for these incidents. In the 2003 CAIR report, complaints were categorised by the environment in which they occurred. Fifteen per cent of these complaints occurred in schools, second only to the workplace.

These statistics and numbers reflect harrowing anecdotal reports of bias, discrimination and violence, often involving minors. On September 17 2003, the *New York Times* reported an incident in which a boy punched a 14-year-old Muslim girl in the face, while verbally abusing her (Dewan, 2003). CAIR reported that in

November 2001, a 4-year-old Muslim girl was threatened by a schoolmate who said he was going to shoot her, after he saw her mother, who wears hijab. In April 2004, CAIR reported another incident in which a 12-year-old girl was attacked with a belt by four teenaged boys, who called her 'Osama.'

Children are not the only ones attacking and harassing Muslim students in schools. CAIR reported that in February 2003, a teacher in Louisiana pulled a headscarf off a student and said,

> I hope God punishes you. No, I'm sorry, I hope Allah punishes you. I didn't know you had hair under there.

Just months later, in October 2003, a Florida bus driver refused to drive Muslim children home from school, forcing them to walk the five miles to their homes.

Religion in American public education

While it is clear that religion, religious bias and Islamophobia are present in US society and schools, school staff or curricula seldom address issues regarding religion.

The United States relationship with the issue of religion in the public schools has been long and often difficult. From the beginning of public schooling in colonial times, the role of religion in public education has been evolving. Today it is governed by US law. In the US Constitution, the supreme law of the country, there is a provision known as the First Amendment, which states that the government shall not establish a religion and shall remain separate from religion. This law applies to actions taken by the 50 states through the Fourteenth Amendment to the Constitution, including public schools which are funded in part by state and federal government.

The courts have been at the centre of the struggle over religion in the public schools. US courts have dealt with disputes over prayer in schools, whether students could have released time on premises for religious education, whether ceremonial bible reading and school sponsored group prayer is allowed and under what conditions (Michaelsen, 1970). Even today, US courts continue to wrestle with high profile issues that directly relate to religion in public schools, such as the recitation of the Pledge of Allegiance – which includes the words 'under God' – in schools, and vouchers that allocate public government funds to support attendance at private schools which are often religiously affiliated.

On one aspect of this debate, however, the courts have not wavered. Public schools may teach about religion. Justice Tom Clark wrote for *Abington v. Schempp*, a famous United States Supreme Court case regarding religion and schools, decided in 1963:

> It might well be said that one's education is not complete without a study of comparative religion or the history of religion and its relationship to the advancement of civilisation. It certainly may be said that the Bible is worthy of study for its literary and historic qualities. Nothing we have said here indicates that such study of the Bible or of religion, when presented objectively as part of a secular programme of education, may not be affected consistently with the First Amendment. (Haynes and Thomas, 2001 p72).

Teaching about religion is legal in the United States. It is encouraged by educational experts. Notwithstanding the legal precedents that permit and even encourage public schools to teach about religion, there is a general fear of any discussion of religion in school, due partly to the complicated and visible history of religion in public schools. Many schools have overly stringent policies, in an unnecessary effort to avoid legal difficulties. Likewise, educators often shy away from any discussion of religion in the classroom for fear of being sanctioned by school administration or having to confront anger from parents. A student at New York University recently shared with her peers in a graduate presentation on education that,

> The teacher I'm working with told me that we are not allowed to address religion with the children at all, even if they ask a question. I have to be really careful about the books I pick out. Any mention of any holiday could be inappropriate. (Finklestein, 2003)

Another reason that religion is rarely addressed by school curricula is the increasing emphasis on preparing students for working life. At the end of the 19th century, American schools began to shift away from helping students to become democratic citizens toward passing on knowledge that would allow students to succeed economically. The emergence of the scientific method and technology also had a secularising effect on modern education (Nord and Haynes, 1998).

Teaching about religion

Regardless of historically ingrained fears or periodic shifts in emphasis in public education, it is not only legal but also necessary to teach children about religion. As presented in Haynes and Thomas (2001), The National Council for the Social Studies asserts:

> Knowledge about religions is not only characteristic of an educated person, but is also absolutely necessary for understanding and living in a world of diversity. (74)

Children must be prepared by their education to actively and positively participate in a democratic society which is among the most diverse in the world.

While Islamophobia and anti-Muslim incidents are indeed disturbing, they are hardly surprising. We are in a society where most people are taught nothing about Islam while being bombarded by the media with sensationalised, negative images of Arabs and Muslims. These images are often targeted at children. For example, in Disney's animated feature, Aladdin, the protagonist characters have light skin and American accents whereas the villains are darkskinned and have Middle Eastern accents. Lyrics to songs in the movie encapsulate the negativity towards Arab culture:

> Oh I come from a land, from a faraway place, where the caravan camels roam. Where they cut off your ear if they don't like your face, it's barbaric, but hey, it's home. (Wingfield and Karaman, 1995)

Children are exposed to such negative images in movies such as True Lies, Back to the Future and Raiders of the Lost Ark and comic books such as Tarzan and Superman. Regardless of the diversity within Muslim culture, Muslims are most often portrayed as Arabs, specifically Arab terrorists, 'oil sheiks' and tribesmen. Female Muslims are presented as 'belly dancers and harem girls.' Positive and unstereotypical images of Muslims are rarely found in the media (Wingfield and Karaman, 1995).

Third graders who were being introduced to the *Building Blocks for Democracy: Children Celebrate their Traditions* programme illustrated this lack of appropriate information in a discussion that took place shortly after 9/11 in a New York City classroom. The children said they received a great deal of their information from television and asked questions like: 'The people who did this believed they could go to heaven but how can you go to heaven if you kill all those people and yourself?' 'How could a religion say that it is OK to hurt people?' The children had no knowledge about Islam and expressed incorrect beliefs, such as that all Muslims speak Arabic and come from the Middle East.

Teaching about religion is also important because knowledge of the world's religions is essential to understand history, literature and current events. One could not begin to understand the complexities of such diverse subjects as the conflict in Northern Ireland, the women's suffrage movement, and James Joyce's *Ulysses* without a basic education in religion. But teaching about different religious traditions is only part of what needs to be done to prepare children to face a religiously diverse and often religiously biased society. As well as knowledge, children also need skills. To thrive in a diverse society and to be prepared to combat prejudice, one needs to be able to understand one's own identity, ask important and respectful questions about others, and find enrichment, not threat, in diversity. These are basic, social-emotional skills, which can be built into the classroom setting.

Educating our youngest citizens

The time to begin teaching these civic, social-emotional skills and to prepare children to learn about the religions of the world is at the very start of formal education, for both developmental and academic reasons. Prejudice and bias do not afflict only adolescents and adults. Research indicates that children can exhibit racist attitudes as early as preschool (Aboud and Fenwick, 1999). Even toddlers can form negative prejudices in an environment that displays 'clear ethnic friction' (Cameron *et al*, 2001, p.124). These writers refer to the Bar-Tal study, in which Israeli children as young as two and a half rated a photograph of a person more negatively when told that the person was Arab.

Even in environments where ethnic friction is not as pervasive, children go through two important social cognitive transitions that affect their formation of prejudice in the early elementary grades of primary school. The first transition is the attainment of racial constancy: children begin to understand that 'they are a member of a racial group that is unchanging over time and across superficial transformations' (Cameron *et al*, 2001, p.124). This transition affects preferences and behaviours, including the way children view themselves and others and seek information about their identity and occurs around the age of five.

The second transition occurs between the ages of seven and nine, when 'children show a qualitatively different understanding of person traits, shifting from primarily physical and concrete to internal and psychological' (*ibid*, p.124). This is also when children can begin to examine 'dispositional characteristics with long-lasting implications (i.e. abilities) rather than simple outcome comparisons' (*ibid*).

During these two transitions children are acquiring critical skills and attitudes about racial, ethnic and religious differences. They are learning about their identity, creating their views of others and beginning to ask questions about culture, race, ethnicity, religion and identity. These are key times in the development of prejudices, because they relate to how a child learns to assign value and judgment on themselves and others. So it is important to address issues of multiculturalism and interreligious understanding during the early stages of a child's development. It is an important time to expand their worldviews and knowledge of cultures.

The early school years are also a critical time for learning about race, ethnicity, religion and culture because these issues tie directly into the academic content children are learning. Kindergarten curricula often incorporate children's names, families and preferences. Later the local community is often studied. Children learn about their cities and towns, their states and cultures around the world. Just as knowledge of religion is necessary for older students to understand international conflict and great literature, it is also important to understanding elementary school curricula about self, community and culture.

A dearth of programming

It is for both academic and developmental reasons that educational programming for the early elementary school child should include both content and skill building around issues of culture, ethnicity, race and religion. But although this kind of programming exists in many forms for secondary school children, there is a dearth of educational materials for the early grades. One organisation that does offer programming for the early elementary grades is the Tanenbaum Center for Interreligious Understanding based in New York City.

The Tanenbaum Center is a non-sectarian, secular, non-profit organisation. Founded in 1992, its programmes build interreligious understanding and thereby strive to defuse the verbal and physical violence done in the name of religion. To that end, it creates practical programmes that enhance everyday lives. One of the practical programmes created by the organisation is *Building Blocks for Democracy: Children Celebrate their Traditions*, a curricular programme for children in the primary grades.

When Building Blocks was first conceived, the Tanenbaum Center worked in partnership with the Union Theological Seminary and the Institute for Christian and Islamic Studies and Relations. The first step was to gather a core group of experts in the fields of religion and education to delineate the goals of the project, which were: to create a positive foundation for mutual respect, to enhance knowledge and awareness of cultural and religious legacies, to reduce prejudice and stereotyping and to create new educational materials that support the Tanenbaum Center's mission and can be used in formal and informal, secular and religious educational settings. The core group undertook research to identify a representative sample of materials available in the field. This research, combined with information gathered from focus groups of teachers, leading educational experts and developmental psychologists, revealed the dearth of educational programming for elementary school children that is multicultural and interreligious, or that promotes the values of respect and inclusion while expanding worldviews.

The core group discovered that the programming and resources that do exist generally fall into one of two categories: programming for secondary education or programming that advocates, but does not necessarily provide curricula for, teaching about religion in schools. Programming is available for older students on the other hand. For example, Facing History and Ourselves in Boston provides a quality curricular programme for high school students. Also, the innovative Three Rs programme in California and Utah seeks to advocate the role of religion in the curriculum to educators in those states.

Building Blocks for Democracy: children celebrate their traditions

Building Blocks for Democracy was designed to fill the gap at the primary school level. The mission of the curricula is to help children establish respectful communities where inclusion and pluralism are valued. The programme offers a menu of curricula that educators are trained to use. Themes covered by Building Blocks curricula range from the Olympic games to community building, to religious traditions around the world. These curricula are designed to prepare children for the civic and social responsibilities of citizenship in a strong democratic society. Since children in the early elementary grades are not ready to learn complete, detailed and abstract histories of the world's religions or how to conduct themselves within the intricacies of a working democracy, Building Blocks prepares the young children for these lessons, which they will encounter later.

The curricula prepare students by teaching them the basic skills that underpin democracy and multiculturalism: communication, respect, inclusion, personal responsibility and participation in community. Children are also introduced to an initial discussion of ethnicity, religion and the study of culture, to stretch their worldviews and prepare them to encounter difference and confront bias. Educators who use the curricula are given substantial staff training on issues of pluralism in the classroom, multiculturalism, pedagogy and the best practices for implementing the curricula. The educators then have access to Building Blocks staff throughout the year for on and off site support, questions and continuing guidance.

Content integration

The Building Blocks curricula are fully integrated into the general curriculum of the elementary school. They are arranged thematically and include lessons in literacy, mathematics, social studies, research, technology, science and art. Other programmes that address issues of respect and multiculturalism are often extracurricular, so are presented during the school day but separately from the general academic curriculum. Presenting these themes to children in a special or separate fashion sends the message that the content is somehow other, separate or less important than the academic lessons taught in the classroom. It is therefore more effective to integrate these lessons in a holistic way so that children learn to value the skills of citizenship and the diversity of cultures, and see them as an important and natural part of everyday life.

The Building Blocks curricula include lessons in diverse subject areas, to assure that children with diverse skill sets and strengths can be successful and valued within the school community. According to Howard Gardner's theory of multiple intelligences, there is not one single type of intelligence but rather eight different types: linguistic, musical, logical-mathematical, spatial, bodily kinaesthetic, interpersonal, intrapersonal and naturalist. Including lessons that develop all these intelligences balances the academic content and all children have the opportunity to shine and to be challenged. Placing value on different types of intelligence and different strengths is an important feature of a programme designed to explore and embrace difference.

Developmental appropriateness

One major challenge in creating educational programming that deals with issues of citizenship, multiculturalism and interreligious understanding in the primary grades is developmental appropriateness. All are abstract concepts, and elementary school students are typically concrete thinkers. So when developing the Building Blocks curricula, it was necessary to present these abstract ideas in concrete ways. One way this was achieved was through concrete, visual examples. For example, in one lesson about citizenship and community, the children make a puzzle. Each child creates his or her own piece of the puzzle and then the class fits the pieces together. The puzzle gives the children a visual and physical representation of how people can fit together, work together and rely on each other to make a whole, as in a community. A writing component of the lesson also teaches academic skills.

Another way in which developmental appropriateness is addressed is through children's literature. Narratives told from a child's perspective are used to introduce children to different traditions and experiences in an accessible way. This not only allows children to access information, it also helps them associate what they are learning about different cultures with real children, with whom they can identify.

Children's stories are written and produced by the Tanenbaum Center for the programme. These stories are about holiday celebrations and family traditions from around the world, both religious and secular. In each, a child narrates their role in the tradition and shares their feelings about it. For example, one little girl describes her favourite dishes and the people who visit her home during Eid Ul-Fitr, as well as explaining the roots of the tradition. Published trade books are also incorporated into the curricula, sych as *The Three Muslim Festivals* by Aminah Ibrahim Ali, which presents Ramadan, Eid Ul-Fitr and Eid Ul-Adha through the eyes of children from three diverse Muslim families.

Citizenship and democracy are similarly abstract concepts that can be difficult to present to young, concrete thinkers. Accordingly the curricula identify and present the skills and conceptual framework for citizenship in concrete, developmentally appropriate ways. For example, the Building Blocks curricula involve students in appropriate interviewing and teach children how to ask respectful questions. One such lesson is the Tell-Me-More activity and this is implemented when the children share their writing. The children write storybooks about their favourite family traditions and then read the stories aloud to the class. After each child reads, the other children are encouraged to ask questions, starting with the phrase, 'tell me more.' An appropriate question could be 'tell me more, Rasheed, what do you wear on Christmas?' Children are helped to ask respectful questions by giving the linguistic tools to do so. It also teaches them what they should not ask: for example, questions or comments that are judgemental, such as 'Rasheed, why don't you eat turkey on Christmas like everyone else?' or 'opening your presents in the morning is stupid'.

In another activity that teaches children how to ask appropriate questions, the educator interviews a religious expert (an adult practitioner of a given religion) in front of the class. After this modelling, the children interview each other. This not only illustrates to the children how to ask appropriate questions and offers them the words and linguistic tools to ask the questions, it also exposes them to the religious tradition of the expert.

A core concept that children learn is that one can only speak from a first person, personal perspective and should not assume the practice, feeling or thinking of others. In the Kaleidoscope activity the children make their own kaleidoscopes. As the children look into their kaleidoscopes, the teacher helps them reflect on the difference between what they see and what another child may see in his or her toy. This helps give the children a concrete metaphor for the concept that each of us can only speak of their personal perspective and experience and can not assume the perspective or experience of another. In a following discussion, the children are then encouraged to say, 'during Eid Ul-Fitr, I visit with my family' rather than, 'during Eid Ul-Fitr, people visit with their families' and begin to learn that not everyone practices, feels and thinks the same way.

Students also engage in discourse around fairness and participate in rule making and voting in the classroom. At the beginning of each school year, students in the Building Blocks programme create their own classroom rules of respect.

Cooperative Learning

A major pedagogical underpinning of the Building Blocks curricula is the use of cooperative learning. Having children talk to and learn from each other is an effective way to have the children practice using their newly acquired skills of communication. It also allows the children to test their citizenship skills, as they are required to work together to create projects and solve problems.

Another benefit of cooperative learning is that it allows the children to act as both teacher and learner and offers ample and rich opportunities for the children to articulate what they have learned. It gives the children an opportunity to benefit and learn from the diversity among their peers. Just as children learn about different cultures and traditions from children in books, they learn from the children they share a classroom with.

Studies have shown that using a peer-education/cooperative learning model in the classroom can also be effective in reducing prejudice in students. Frances E. Aboud and Virginia Fenwick's *Exploring and Evaluating School-Based Interventions to Reduce Prejudice* (1999) examined a study that compared teacher directed instruction and peer socialisation. They found that 'the collaborative framework ensured that students were engaged, open in expressing their views, and intent on explaining and evaluating their views' and could be more effective in reducing prejudice than didactic teacher-led instruction.

To use this model effectively, however, an educator must be properly trained. In fact, peer education is a vital part of the educator training given to the educators who implement the Building Blocks programme. While children have much to learn from one another, and need to communicate with their peers to hone their communication skills, an effective educator must know when it is his or her role to step in or, if necessary, to take over the conversation. For example, if a child is heard making biased or disrespectful comments, it is imperative that the educator immediately address the situation, by refuting the statements with examples and identifying the source of the comments.

Community Involvement and Service

Another important tenet of the Building Blocks programme is community involvement. Each academic year culminates with a special event at which the community comes together to share and celebrate the children's learning. Community service is another way that Building Blocks involves children in the community and an important component of preparing children to become active and positive citizens in a pluralistic society. It also helps the children explore the cultural diversity within their environment.

Involving the students with the community helps connect the children to the support system that the greater community offers. Becoming aware of the role of community allows the children to see themselves as an important part of a larger whole. This is an integral concept within citizenship, as it is the foundation of personal responsibility and civic duty. Having the children conduct community service projects can help the children identify and work on issues of social justice and allow them to feel empowered. Community service projects allow children to be leaders, teachers, achievers and powerful members of a community, all while experiencing the real world applications of their academic learning. Community service can also bring people of different religions and traditions together to share their similarities. Many different traditions, including Islam, Judaism, Hinduism and Christianity include elements of service. Service can therefore be both studied and performed as a commonality or a shared value in a pluralistic society.

Successful community service projects go beyond simply providing a service. Ideal service projects are those that serve the community and develop the child. Service learning should incorporate academic learning as it is applied in real-life situations. For example, if children are involved in a project at a soup kitchen, there should be ample opportunities for learning about nutrition, hands-on learning about food science and an extension into social studies regarding issues of class (social justice). There should also be opportunities to develop the child's sense of values and caring. Working directly with people in need at the soup kitchen is more likely to accomplish this than textbook learning or a classroom-based project. An ideal service project also allows for self-reflection and self-discovery. In the Building Blocks Community Building curricula, the children first read a book about a girl who identified a problem in her community and began to solve it. The children are then challenged with finding something in their community that could be improved, and brainstorm a way to make appropriate improvements. The children participate in action planning before the work and evaluation during and after. Through this project, the children reflect critically on their surroundings and their abilities. They use and develop planning skills, connect to their community and begin to take ownership of an issue that affects them. Effective service work should engage and challenge students in this way.

Experiences and challenges

One of the major challenges of the implementation of Building Blocks is working with educators who are fearful about addressing religion with their students. Building Blocks staff works with a wide variety of schools and educational settings, including public, private and independent schools as well as after-school programmes. The fears about religion in school are not unique to public educators. Educators in private settings, where the federal laws may not apply, also feel apprehensive about addressing this sensitive subject in the classroom. Our staff has therefore identified a need for teacher training, which would begin with a focus on the legalities involved with religion in the public school, including the First Amendment of the United States Constitution, which states:

> Congress shall make no law respecting an establishment of religion, or prohibiting the free exercise thereof; or abridging the freedom of speech, or of the press; or the right of the people peaceably to assemble, and to petition the government for a redress of grievances.

Because educators have indicated that their concerns about talking about religion often come from parents and administrators, training often extends to school leadership and can be provided to the greater community as well. Another concern that educators sometimes report about using the Building Blocks curricula is that they are already under substantial curricular demands. In the age of standards based reform, teachers work according to stringent policies about what they need to teach and are subject to increased standardised testing and measures of accountability. In some areas, like New York City, the government mandates entire curricula. Teachers, and even administrators, do not always have the freedom to choose curricula and even those who do may be hesitant, as they are under so many other mandates and demands. Consequently, our staff not only works with individual schools and educators, but also identify key partnerships that help to advocate and disseminate the programme.

Even when there has been anxiety during the initial phase of implementation, the programme usually flourishes and expands. When Building Blocks began to work in after-school sites of the YMCA of Greater New York, there was an initial agreement to put the programme in a limited number of sites. One year later, after a successful pilot period, the YMCA has written letters of endorsement. It has conducted a joint fundraising effort with the Tanenbaum Center and is working to put Building Blocks in all of its academic after-school programmes.

Individual educators who begin tentatively with the programme see it grow with them. It is the reactions of the children to the programme that are the strongest and most poignant indicators of success. Teachers have reported children behaving more inclusively across social and ethnic groups on the playground and in the classroom. They have also indicated that the children become excited about the programme, and initiate their own research about different cultures. Further evidence of success is seen in the classroom rules the children generate themselves such as: treat others as you want to be treated, cooperate with others, and be sure of yourself.

Sometimes, the most powerful evidence of success is the cessation of incidents. At East Moriches Elementary School in New York, the principal reported the following story to the Building Blocks staff. East Moriches is an elementary school whose population is fairly homogeneous, made up of mostly Caucasian, Christian students. Muslim students are a small minority. One Muslim student had been attending school in Western dress. Upon puberty, she began to wear hijab and more modest and traditional clothing. The change of dress was met without incident and the school administration and staff attributed the success to Building Blocks because the programme had exposed children at East Moriches to Muslim culture – among others – in a positive way and taught them to ask questions about religion appropriately and respectfully (Leeds, 2004).

Conclusion

Increasing Islamophobia is a disturbing trend in the United States today. Combating Islamophobia and any religious bias begins with the preparation of our youngest citizens. While there are few programmes that address issues of cultural and religious bias with elementary school students, even our youngest children must be appropriately prepared to face a religiously diverse and often religiously biased society. From the earliest age, this involves both educating students about different religions and cultures and teaching the necessary skills for living in a pluralistic and democratic society.

Building Blocks for Democracy: Children Celebrate their Traditions is a unique programme that prepares children in this way. The programme exposes young children to cultures and religions they may not normally encounter in a culturally and developmentally appropriate way, while simultaneously teaching both academic and social skills. Through peer-education, academic activities, children's literature, and community service projects, children learn how to celebrate pluralism. While elementary school students are unprepared for complex and abstract information about religious devotion or conflict, they are ready to learn to talk to one another about special traditions, practice asking respectful questions, serve and connect with their communities, explore cultures, dismiss stereotypes and express their own identities. Building Blocks is a programme that helps them do this in a practical way.

7

Muslims in Italy: social changes and educational practices

Michele Bertani

Italian Islam: a multinational and multiethnic presence

I n only a few years, Italy has become a country of immigration after long being a country of emigration. From the early 1800s until the early 1960s, hundreds of thousands of Italian emigrants left their country for the challenge of a new life in America, Australia or Northern Europe. Over the last thirty years, however, Italy has seen profound demographic changes: the slowing internal flow of people from the South to the North, decreased emigration, growth in the population-age ratio, and declining birth rates. At the end of 2002, the foreign population in Italy was estimated to be around one and half million out of a total population of nearly sixty million. The ethnic, religious and national character of these immigrants among the most heterogeneous in Europe.

The presence of migrants in Italy who have their roots in Arab countries is a recent phenomenon. The Italian Islamic community is represented by numerous nationalities and ethnicities. The most represented country of origin is Morocco (170,500), followed by Albania (109,000). The nearly 700,000 immigrants from other Islamic countries hail from Northern Africa, West Africa, the

Middle East and Asia. Islam has become the second most practised religion in Italy after Catholicism.

Migrant communities are typically organised through practical and social networks linked to their ethnic and national origins. Consequently religious traditions and practices vary among communities. We can observe three main types of Islamic communities in Europe at the moment: practising believers, traditionalists and those who have become secularised. The last category, according to Tariq Ramadan (2002, p256), are those 'Muslims without Islam, the ones who consider the message of Islam in terms of theoretical values and good moral intentions.'

According to Allam and Gritti (2001, p25):

> Italian Islam [is] characterised by different religious nuances and a natural diversity in the way people associate. It is important to observe how the Muslim population has not developed closed enclaves such as we can find in the UK. A confirmation of this statement can be identified in the diffusion of Muslims in different urban areas. French-style *banlieus* do not exist in Italy and immigrant citizens are scattered throughout the Italian population. We can find immigrants of Muslim origin in the downtown areas of cities, in small villages or in the countryside.

Muslim leaders and Italian society: analysis of the interactions

If we examine the public identity of Muslims in Italy today, however, we discover less diversity. Only a limited number of religious associations fulfil the role of public representatives and a small number of Islamic Councils manage religious life through the mosques. Some leaders of these Islamic organisations have gained celebrity status and publicly reinforce the stereotypes of a strong and aggressive Islam. With the complicity of the media, who give them constant visibility and space, such leaders tend to promote themselves as the representatives of the entire Muslim community in Italy.

The few radical Islamic leaders who regularly appear on television seem to exploit the lack of knowledge of Islam in the media and their need for an audience. Although these two or three leaders represent only a minority of the Muslim population, they are, thanks to the media, seen as representing the entire Muslim community. Recently, one of these leaders invited the Pope to convert to Islam, while another voiced his support for the views of Osama bin Laden on the Western world. The Islamic establishment has itself often criticised such comments. Nevertheless, it is the radical statements that have been considered newsworthy. This has had negative consequences for public opinion of Islam and Muslims.

Local representatives of Islamic religious associations have worked hard as intermediaries in their communities, leading some experts to call them the 'intense minority' (Guolo, 2003, p6). The majority of Muslims in Italy, however, quietly maintain their cultural and traditional faith, often praying at home.

So who does represent Muslims in Italy? What is the role of the *Unione delle Comunità e Organizzazioni Islamiche in Italia* (Union of Islamic Organisations and Communities in Italy) or the *Lega Musulmana mondiale – sezione Italia* (Italian Branch of the World Muslim League)? An important authority on the issue, like Tariq Ramadan (2002, p198), writes that presently only 15 per cent of European Muslims regularly attend a mosque. This means that a high percentage of Muslims are not directly represented by religious associations. The largest group are the so-called 'silent Muslims' (Saint-Blancat, 1997, pp123-128). These are women, Sufi Muslims and those who use their Islamic roots as a cultural and social reference, but do not practice their faith openly.

The growth of Islamophobia

As in other Western nations, attitudes towards the Muslim community as well as other national, ethnic and religious minorities changed after the terrorist attacks in New York on September 11, 2001. The studies carried out between September 2001 and January 2002 showed a slight rise in intolerance towards Muslims. The results did show that a small group of those interviewed perceived Muslims as a threat to Italian national culture and identity. However, anti-Islam sentiment is not new. The idea of Islam as a menace was supported by several political groups even before September 11th.

The change in public attitudes toward Muslims was confirmed by an ISPO/Nielsen study[1] conducted on October 21, 2001. Those sampled answered as follows:

ISPO/Nielsen study

Is Islam intolerant?
Yes 43%
No 24%
Don't know 33%

Can Arabs be trusted?
Yes 38%
No 36%
Don't know 26%

Should immigrants of Arab Muslim origin leave Italy?
Yes 25%
No 46%
Don't know 29%

Should we accept Christian and turn back Muslim immigrants?
Yes 9% (April 2001)
Yes 13% (the same question on October 2001)

Some of the events that might have changed the attitudes of the Italian public were:

• Statements by a few Italian politicians and opinion leaders, who presented Islam and foreigners in general as a threat to Italian culture and traditions.

• Provocative statements made by activist *a'imma* (plural for Imam), who live in Italy, and who subsequently received significant media attention. These *a'imma* were portrayed as spokespersons for the Islamic community as a whole, though they were often criticised by the most important leaders of their own communities.

• The copious news concerning investigations into *Al Qaeda* supporters in Italy and the constant messages by authorities warning of possible terrorist attacks. Newspapers and television spoke of potential attacks in which the presumed targets were to be Italian highways during the summer season. Public authorities also talked of possible risks during the Christmas holidays.

- The frequent appearance in public fora of radical Muslim leaders who do not represent the entire community. In this way, public opinion received a distorted or only partial image of Islam.

The survey item referring to the acceptance of immigrants with Christian origins (mostly from Eastern Europe) versus rejecting those with an Islamic background, has found support on the Italian political agenda in the last couple of years. Acts of racism and violence towards Muslims increased between September and December of 2001, the period in which the media included the most news items and feature stories about Islam and Islam-related issues. Though acts of direct violence seem to have been limited, hidden racism and intolerance has grown. Such covert developments might be even more dangerous because they are commonly accepted as a shared world view. This underlying intolerance is different from overt attacks or acts of violence which are condemned unanimously by public opinion.

Examples of 'light' racism reported by media have included:

- the young Italian Muslim girl who had to leave her veil at home in order to be able to work in an attorney's office

- the motion passed by a Provincial District in Northern Italy that terminated the employment of workers with Arab Muslim origins

- the city council decision in Northeast Italy to close a mosque because it violated health standards

- the motion presented by a political group in Parliament to cut off finances for a mosque in Naples

- the declaration by a major national magazine that Oriana Fallaci is the most important Italian writer, thereby legitimating her strongly derogatory comments about Islam.

The Crucifix in the state school controversy

A recent incident in Italy which gained international attention is worth discussing in detail because it provides insights into the difficulty of confronting Islamophobia and developing tolerance towards a minority faith in a country where one religion has been dominant for many centuries. The controversy, dubbed by the media the 'Crisis of the Crucifix', became national and international news after a judgement issued by the Court of L'Aquila on October 2003. The court demanded the removal of the Crucifix from two classrooms in a local state school – one in a nursery school classroom and another in a primary school classroom. A controversial Islamic activist (Adel Smith) had started legal proceedings against the school attended by his sons. At the beginning of the school year, Smith was permitted by teachers to display a small picture representing the *sura* 112 of the Koran in the classroom attended by his children. The school's principal had it removed shortly thereafter. During the same month, Smith sought advice from the Court in the municipality where he lives (L'Aquila), asserting that the presence of a Crucifix in public spaces, such as in a state school, goes against the principle of respect for different religious beliefs and equal treatment, as granted by the Italian Constitution. The Court's decision in his favour gave rise to numerous reactions and debates, both at the institutional level and in public opinion. For many weeks, television and newspapers reported on the issue. Ministries, politicians and experts took strong positions on the decision. Below are some quotes from these authority figures.

> I respect the Court's decision, but I feel hurt as a Christian and a citizen. The Crucifix is not only the symbol of my religion but also the ultimate display of 2,000 years of civilisation, which belongs to the Italian people[2] (Giuseppe Pisanu, Ministry for Internal Affairs)

> Any judge who expresses such excessive comments is liable to sanctions. I am going to inform the Ministerial Inspectors to verify if the decision was issued in accordance with the legal system or if the rules were ignored[3] (Roberto Castelli, Ministry of Justice)

> The Crucifix in the classroom is the civic value symbol of our country. The interpretation of the Law by a judge can not deny the same rules. Therefore, I invite the legal adviser of the State and the

Ministry of Education to apply to the authorities for the protection of the Law[4] (Luca Volontà, Member of Parliament and representative of UDC Party)

I do not understand the legal tenet used for the Court's decision. It is not possible to remove the symbol of the religious and cultural values of our nation only because it might cause trouble for someone. I think this path is dangerous. Why we do not remove churches or stop the usually humanitarian aims of the Red Cross?[5] (Ersilio Tonini, Archbishop of Ravenna)

The Ministry of Education appealed against the Court's decision on November 30, 2003. Only a few lines in the newspapers reported the second decision of the Court to revoke its initial decision because it felt it had no competence to decide on the matter.

Italian laws regarding religion

Section 1, p. 1 of the Law of 25 March 1985 abrogates the principles of Catholicism as the official State religion. The article was a consequence of the amendment to the *Concordato* (the treaty between the Italian State and the Vatican), and the realisation of the principles laid out in Article 7 of the Republican Constitution, which states that the Italian Republic and the Catholic Church, each with its own legal status, are independent and sovereign entities.

The *Consiglio di Stato* (Court of Appeal for administrative justice, sentence 63/88 – April 1988) declared that 'the Crucifix represents the symbol of Christian civilisation and culture in its historical roots, as being universal and independent of any specific religious faith'. The Ministry of Education issued a directive[6] on October 2002 regarding the display of the Crucifix in classrooms. The directive stated that Royal Decrees dating back to 1924 and 1928 are still in effect and that the Principal of any school must verify that the Holy symbol is displayed in school.

The Ministry's directive does, however, contain a proposal that asks educational institutions to create 'space or rooms for meditation' that should be open to a school's students and teaching staff. According to the Ministry, these spaces, which are in fact prayer rooms, need to respect 'several religious faiths' that attend Italian schools, including Muslim students and teachers. According to Guolo (2003, p141),

> The proposal of the Ministry confuses education with faith. Prayer is not one of the aims of the state school. Teachers' educational practices and lectures should show respect for different religions. This project [could generate religious conflicts] in a place where compassion and sharing should be the values.

Public debate led to the presentation of a bill presented on May 15 2002 by a group of Parliamentarians that mandates the display of the Crucifix in all public facilities (including classrooms, courtrooms, hospitals, railway stations, bus stations, airports, jails). According to the provisions of this bill, those failing to do so could face fines up to 1000 EURO or up to six months imprisonment. The Italian Jewish community has taken issue with this directive, arguing that it could lead to a clash of civilisations and various forms of intolerance. The bill is presently being examined by the Parliament's Constitutional Affairs Commission.

The judgment by Judge M. Montanaro, Court of L'Aquila, October 22, 2003

Let us return to the judgment that allowed the Principal to remove the Crucifix in the classrooms attended by the two young Muslim students in L'Aquila. Judge M. Montanaro wrote:

> The unequivocal abrogation of the principle that Catholicism is the State religion, amended by section 1, p. 1 of the Law 25 in March 1985, introduced a new structure that runs counter to the regulations that call for the Crucifix to be displayed. The rules which demand this, moreover at a secondary level and linked to the principle of the State religion, must be repealed.

Italy, as a sovereign state, both in the past and today, has always had peculiar relations with the Vatican. Judge Montanaro's judgment highlights the fact that the Constitution affirms the independence of both the Italian State and the Catholic Church. It thus acknowledges that state religion does not exist. In daily life, however, Catholicism is often considered to be the state religion of Italy.

The public debate

The Court's judgment provoked a strong outcry, which was magnified by the media. Part of the media blitz is perhaps explained by the fact that the activist who brought the case to the Court was renowned for his openly anti-Christian remarks. The general public responded with fear and worry, and the common response was that the judgment represented a menace to Christian identity and culture. Interestingly, a similar request to remove the Crucifix from classrooms attended by atheists or non-Catholic students had been presented to Courts in previous years, but did not excite such intense protest or public debate as the 'crisis of the Crucifix' in October 2003.

In January 2004, the administrative Court in Venice issued a judgment after an appeal by the atheist parents of two children. Their demand had also been to remove the Crucifix in the children's classrooms. The Court in Venice stated that the existing rules 'seem to provide an advantage to Catholics, giving concessions that are not justified according to the Constitution, even if Catholicism is the most practised religion in Italy.' The Court of Venice suspended its verdict, however, leaving the final decision to the Constitutional Court. The media paid little attention to this judgment: only a few lines about it appeared in one national newspaper. One can ask if this was the consequence of the petitioners being unknown atheists instead of a well-known Islamic activist?

Even the Islamic community was split on the controversy in L'Aquila. Below are two quotes from representatives of the moderate Islamic community who indicate a desire to avoid conflict and live together in harmony with the majority community.

> The Crucifix or the discussion about celebrating Christmas in the classroom is not a problem. And I think it will not generate any problem for my little child when she will attend school. Because I will explain to her what the meaning of Christmas is and what the Crucifix represents for our Christians brothers.[7] (Mohammed Guerfi, *imam* of the Islamic Council in Verona)

> What do I think about the demand to remove the Crucifix? This initiative upsets and shocks me because it demonstrates the absence of respect for Italian traditions and faith. Moreover, it is an

absurd idea to create a sort of religious space for Muslims who are overly sensitive and easily get offended.[8] (Dalil Boubakeur, President of the French Muslim Council and Rector of the Mosque of Paris)

Moving towards solutions: Italian society

There have been several positive developments in Italy in the last couple of years, both in general and more specifically at the educational level. Many opinion leaders have called for Italians to reject the common stereotypes of Islam and to promote the study of Arab Muslim culture, an issue that received little attention in the media before 9/11 because media attention was dominated by immigration issues. Various conferences, debates and public fora on the topic have been organised, at both local and national levels.

Television and newspapers have in some cases aired documentaries or special reports emphasising the pluralistic nature of Islam. This has represented a departure from earlier broadcasts that often portrayed Islam in highly stereotypical ways. One of the most important examples of positive steps that have been taken in Italian society was the call on December 14, 2001 by the Catholic Church for a day of fasting at the end of *Ramadan*. This day of fasting, shared by Muslims and Christians alike, provided the first occasion for a dialogue between the two communities. This dialogue seems necessary to construct a future of peace and cohabitation in a country that will become more and more multiethnic. It is important to avoid ideology and indifference when taking this path.

Moving towards solutions: Italian schools
The changing face of Italian schools

The Ministry of Education, University and Research (MIUR, *Ministero dell'Istruzione, dell'Università e della Ricerca*) in Italy published the document *Alunni con cittadinanza non italiana* (Students without Italian citizenship) in June 2002. The study confirms a constant increase in the number of foreign students in Italian schools. Even though 2.3 per cent foreign students is comparatively lower than other European countries on a national scale, the trend is in line with developments in countries with a longer tradition of immigration, such as France, the United Kingdom, Belgium and Germany. Of the 180,000 foreign students attending Italian schools in June 2001, nearly 40,000 had their roots in Arab countries.

According to Guolo (2003, p133), foreign students face a situation of double isolation: from their native country and from the society in which they live due to incomplete integration. Teachers are not always prepared for this situation. Some pay little or no attention to the new realities in their classrooms and do not seem to be interested in addressing new educational challenges. Others are more motivated, however, to pay attention to the circumstances of these students, often using their personal resources and time to seek additional training. Such efforts can help schools address the new situation in an overall educational context where there are few specific pedagogical remedies.

In the 1990s, the so-called *autonomia scolastica* (school self-government) reforms were introduced. The first measures were implemented in 1997 and outlined two levels of reform:

- national, which provided general descriptions of the learning process and of education in a modern classroom

- local, referring to the place where programmes are implemented in concrete situations in accordance with the criteria proposed by the law

These new reforms leave ample room for local initiatives and are encouraged by professional institutions of learning. As a consequence, it is possible to develop more culturally sensitive programmes in the educational system that promote diversity. Due to this government initiative, it has become possible to develop intercultural projects that create opportunities for debate, discussion and presentations pertaining to the topic of the 'other' in society. For instance, in primary schools teachers can address certain multicultural themes in collaboration with an expert who can introduce the topic of cultural differences using role-plays, stories and tales. Secondary schools focus attention on the importance of dialogue with representatives of different religious communities. While the MIUR Directives underline the importance of protect-

ing foreign students' native cultures, the guidelines for a full intercultural education are frequently general and imprecise. According to Portera (2003, p.x),

> [the establishment] analyses the strategies of intervention, the
> educational programme, and the curricula in a very fast way. The
> results are often negative and the solutions are not suitable in the
> real context.

According to a survey conducted by the MIUR, the number of
foreign students in Italy is estimated to rise to 500,000-700,000 by
2020. Even today, only a small number of such students (5,000)
come from other European Union Member States. There are more
than 32,000 Albanian students and nearly 28,000 Moroccan ones.
If, according to Batelaan (2003), learning to live together means
reciprocal respect of diversity and equality in the relationship, it will
become increasingly important to develop intercultural education
within the Italian school system. The majority of students of Arab
Muslim origin attend state schools. Only a small number attend
Islamic schools, including Libyan schools in Rome and Milan, a
Tunisian school in Mazara del Vallo, and the Islamic Centre's
school in Milan, supervised by the Egyptian authorities. The curricula in these schools are based on Ministry of Education directives
and/or those of the country of origin. There is no discernable
relationship to the local context.

Meeting the needs of Muslim students

Muslim parents who live in Europe tend to be quite protective of
their values and traditions, and it is here that the Italian public
school system has a problem meeting expectations, particularly
those of families that actively practice their religion. Many students
of Arab Muslim origin attend *madrassah* during the weekend,
where they take courses on Arabic languages and Muslim identity
and tradition. These courses are organised by religious or by immigrant associations. There are a variety of programmes and
projects available if one looks at the situation across Italy. In a few
instances, parents can choose between several courses within the
same city (often differing in their level of religiosity). Not surprisingly, the courses organised by mosques stress religious issues and
conformity to traditional values.

Officially, schools owned by religious associations are recognised as private institutions. Article 3 of the Italian Constitution decrees that:

> ...the Law, regarding the rights and duties related to privately-owned schools, must assure that students receive treatment and teaching methods that are equivalent to state owned schools.

Catholic and Jewish state-recognised private schools already exist in Italy. Proposals have recently been made to include Islam as an optional subject in state schools or alternatively to organise general modules on Arab Muslim culture in Autonomous schools. The Italian Islamic establishment is aware of the political difficulties of such moves, especially given the dominant role that Catholicism plays in the Italian public school system. Several associations have been discussing for years how to set up recognised Islamic schools that resemble those that already exist in other European countries. This aim seems more feasible even if quite difficult to achieve in the short term. The Italian Constitution and the Law on privately managed schools makes this possible in the near future. According to Piccardo (1999, p63), the Secretary of the *Unione delle Comunità e Organizzazioni Islamiche in Italia* (Union of the Islamic Organisations and Communities in Italy), the idea exists in the Italian Islamic community to,

> ...create a real state-recognised private school, with teachers able to teach Islamic culture, and their ideas for integration of this culture into Italian society, which will follow the principles of our faith and the long tradition of tolerance. Therefore, our schools will accept students who do not have Arab Muslim heritage.

However, the situation still appears fragmented. There is no solid proposal nor shared project that is backed by the community as a whole, but with each passing day this subject becomes more important, even for Italian society.

Among the developments in the Italian educational system that can be used to promote greater tolerance towards Muslims and other minorities introducing intercultural religious education in teacher training and other government funded training might have greatest effect. It would also offer a positive challenge for Italian Islam. A condition for success, however, is that teaching religion

should require intercultural approaches. According to Portera
(2003, pp. 21-22) such an approach implies

> ...to educate in the faith which everyone has freely decided to join,
> but it is important to underline that it is necessary to include the
> importance of dialogue, respect and the ability to share common
> values with members of different faiths.

An example of good practice

Each year, The *Centro Interculturale 'Millevoci'* ('A thousand voices'
Intercultural Centre) in the Province of Trento, in collaboration
with the *Forum Trentino per la Pace* (Trento Forum for Peace), pro-
poses a series of initiatives and educational projects. The main
objective is to stimulate students to reflect on the themes of peace,
intercultural education and citizenship rights. The Islamic Community of Trentino Alto Adige is one of the associations that participates in this educational project. The collaboration with the
Centro Interculturale 'Millevoci' made it possible to develop a project entitled *'Aprire la scuola al mondo'* (The school meets the
world). This initiative encourages students to focus attention on
other cultures and develop a better understanding of the reality of
'others' who live in their neighbourhood. It also facilitates the
integration of young students who have their roots in other
countries. Representatives of the Islamic Community are invited
to schools to introduce Arab-Islamic history and culture, and to
talk about the traditions and the geography of Arab countries.
Furthermore, guided tours for students and teachers are planned
to the Islamic Community centre of *Trentino Alto Adige*, which is
also the main mosque of the city.

If this type of intercultural educational approach is embraced,
Muslims, as well as adherents to other faiths, will receive the kind
of acknowledgement of their identity and culture that they are
entitled to. This positive challenge would encourage the Muslim
community as a whole, even the 'silent majority', to reflect on their
children's place in Italian society. Italian society needs to participate in this process as a main actor in the dialogue. The search
for 'shared values' (Batelaan and Gundara, 1993, pp61-80) is a
basic element of intercultural education. Such an approach will be
an important step towards the creation of a 'citizenship contract'

(Guolo, 2003, p156) that will help define reciprocal rights and duties for migrants living in European society.

Notes

1 http://www.corriere.it/ October 29 2001, p11

2 *Corriere della Sera*, October 26 2003, on-line edition

3 *Corriere della Sera*, October 26 2003, on-line edition

4 *La Repubblica*, October 26 2003, on-line edition

5 *La Repubblica*, October 25 2003, on-line edition

6 Ministry of Education, Note 3 October 2002 – prot. N. 2667, *Esposizione del crocifisso nelle aule scolastiche*, http://www.istruzione.it/normativa/2002/dir31002.shtml (06/01/2004)

7 *Verona Fedele*, November 18 2001, p3

8 *La Stampa*, October 31 2003, p14

8

Education and Islam:
a new strategy

Maurice Irfan Coles

In the name of God, the Most Gracious, the Ever Merciful

Introduction

This chapter is largely based upon a presentation made to the first English Local Education Authority (LEA) conference specifically designed to address issues related to Islam and education, organised jointly by Leicester City's School Development Support Agency and the University of Leicester in February 2003. In addition, it incorporates some of the findings of an English government Department For Education and Skills (DFES) research project designed to establish the extent and quality of materials reflecting the experience of Muslim pupils (DFES, 2004). It is written to encourage frank, open and honest international discourse about the nature of Islam in the 21st century and the responsibility and contribution Education Services and their partners might make to help shape the debate. It considerably widens the traditional British debate, which centred mainly on the levels of attainment – or more precisely, under-attainment – of the two largest Muslim communities, Pakistani/Kashmiri and Bangladeshis; and on meeting the religious and cultural needs of Muslim pupils. The chapter aims to justify and suggest a strategic approach to addressing educational issues as they relate the Muslim communities.

The rationale for a new strategic approach to Islam and education

Many LEAs and schools, as part of their wider school improvement and race equality strategies, do attempt to address the religious and cultural needs of the range of religious groups that make up the communities they serve. In theory, English schools that are 'maintained' by public money are required to ensure that their implementation of the National Curriculum includes a range of experiences that reflect the country's diversity. Similarly, the English school inspection system, Ofsted, is required to evaluate the effectiveness of such provision. Although there are many similarities with other faith groups, the issues facing British Muslims are different in kind and in degree, and go to the very heart of what it means to be a Muslim in the UK, in Europe and in the world. There are fifteen global, national and local drivers, all of which resonate within the UK context and all of which provide an overwhelming case for devising a new strategic approach.

The rise of Islamophobia

The events of 9/11, the invasions of Afghanistan and Iraq, and various 'terrorist' attacks throughout the world have led to an increase in anti-Muslim sentiment, expression and action. For many Muslims the wearing of hijab, or having beards or turbans, or any dress code that can vaguely be associated with Islam, has provoked overt hostility. Islamophobia is a relatively new term but a very old prejudice. It has little to do with Islam itself but is more about people's prejudiced perceptions of Islam. It was originally coined in the 1980s on an analogy with the word 'xenophobia' (hostility towards foreigners). Historically anti-Muslim feeling has been a feature of European culture since the Crusades. Over time it has been used to justify acts of expansion and aggression against a range of countries and empires. Originally, Muslims were perceived as the enemy outside (the gates), sometimes the enemy at the gate. More recently, with over 10 million Muslim citizens of the European Union, they have become for some 'the enemy within.'

THE FIFTEEN DRIVERS OF THE NEW STRATEGIC APPROACH TO ISLAM AND EDUCATION

1. The evil and tragic events of 9/11 and its continuing aftermath have placed the nature of Islam itself, and the position of its adherents who are citizens of western countries, at the forefront of the agenda of many governments.

2. Faith and the remembrance of God, specifically through a commitment to the teaching of the Messenger Muhammad (PBUH) are the key determinants in the lives of many Muslims. An education system that fails to recognise, acknowledge and build upon this is failing its pupils.

3. The Muslim view of learning and of 'revealed' and 'acquired' knowledge is not understood or utilised positively in the mainstream.

4. The omission of Muslim perspectives from the school curriculum and of genuine recognition of Islamic civilisation serves to undermine the confidence of Muslim pupils, and miseducates non-Muslims by implicitly denying the shared histories and narratives that make up pluralist Britain and pluralist Europe.

5. The serious under-attainment of many Muslim pupils in Britain, particularly those of Pakistani/ Kashmiri and Bangladeshi heritage, requires closer scrutiny and concerted action to close the attainment gap.

6. A robust, frank and open debate about what it means to be a European Muslim is required. This debate should explore the relationship of Islam to citizenship education and will help Muslim pupils of both genders in their own attempts to define their identity (ies) in the 21st century.

7. Closer links between mainstream schools, mosques and madrasahs will benefit all Muslim pupils, help raise attainment in mainstream schools, and support attempts madrasahs may wish to make in changing their pedagogic style.

8. The incorporation of a Muslim frame of reference into all policies will support schools and LEAs in fulfilling their statutory requirements.

9. Effective responses to meeting the needs of Muslim pupils will satisfy some of the requirements outlined in the new Ofsted framework, especially if schools have proactively involved their pupils.

10. A strategic approach which is joined up and coherent across the range of European, national and local government departments will help support the drive for community cohesion and help put an end to the 'parallel lives' and segregation of various communities.

11. The well documented rise of Islamophobia provides an even greater urgency to address these issues.

THE FIFTEEN DRIVERS OF THE NEW STRATEGIC APPROACH TO ISLAM AND EDUCATION continued

12. The rise of Muslim extremism and sectarianism must be addressed openly so that all sectors of society, Muslims and non-Muslims, can engage with them.

13. For the Muslim community (ies), known collectively as the *ummah*, major geo-political issues like the Israel-Palestine conflict, the disputes in Kashmir, the religious strife in Gujarat, and the presence of non-Muslim armies in Iraq and Afghanistan are very real and exist here and now; not merely for the Muslim population but also for such groups as British born Jews, those of Hindu Gujarati origin, and of Punjabi Sikh heritage.

14. Many asylum seekers are of Muslim origin and can suffer the double impact of being despised for seeking asylum and despised for being Muslim.

15. The combination of all these factors has the potential to be the explosive spark that can undermine the very roots of our shared multi-faith, multicultural, multiethnic, pluralist democracy. The very complexity necessitates a well thought out, clearly articulated strategy at school, LEA, national and European level.

The term 'Islamophobia' itself became widely known in Britain after the publication of a report by the Runnymede Trust, *Islamophobia – a challenge for us all*, in 1997. This well argued and balanced report made a clear distinction between legitimate debate and disagreement about Muslim beliefs and customs, a debate in which many Muslims themselves participate and what the authors called 'open views of Islam'; and between what the authors argue is unfounded prejudice and hostility, the 'closed views of Islam'. The report offers a thorough examination of the distinctions they make between these views and argue that an irrational fear of Islam is the recurring characteristic of closed views. The challenge is complex because it involves challenging the misconceptions held by many non-Muslims about the nature of Islam, and challenging the different and often conflicting views held by adherents themselves.

The history of British racism appears to repeat itself in different guises. The arguments that were fought and won – at least by many British schools and authorities – in the 1980s and 90s to persuade schools and LEAs to tackle direct, indirect and institutional racism have now to be restated within an Islamic context. Failure to tackle Islamophobia is another form of miseducation because the alienation it causes wastes talent, causes hurt and grief to the victims and leaves the perpetrators with a false sense of their own superiority. A worldview that sees over 10 million of Europe's population as alien, different, 'the enemy within' is not sustainable in a multicultural, multifaith, inclusive society. Unless tackled systematically, it is likely to breed levels of resentment that do lead to violent resistance which in turn can lead to increased racism as the consequence of such violence. The cycle can and does all too easily repeat itself.

Muslim perspectives

How do Muslims, especially young Muslims, see these issues? The problem for Muslim youth is that Islam is not a homogenous 'one size fits all' religion. Its sectarian and doctrinal divisions are potentially deep and complicated. 'Fundamentalist', anti-Western statements can seem attractive to European Muslim youth, especially those who feel disaffected and disempowered. Britain's Muslims, like Europe's generally, are a 'community of communities'. They can be divided by ethnic, cultural, linguistic and historical factors that often mean that outside their faith background they have little in common. Even within the faith, there can be huge differences between Sunni and Shi'ah, between Barelvis and Deobandis, between the Wahhabis and the Sufis. Mohammad S. Raza, in *Islam in Britain Past, Present and Future*, argues that sectarianism seems to have become serious in Britain. It has become so, he believes, because many Muslims are reacting to a predominantly secular society in which they fear they will lose their children to 'Western' values. Their response is to cling to sectarian affiliations that in turn have increased rivalries, which defeats one of the purposes of being a Muslim, that is of being a united community (Raza, 1993).

The Ummah

The great irony is that the Muslim community, although divided in many ways, does see itself as a community, as the Ummah. It is perhaps difficult for a non-Muslim to appreciate the degree of commonality and the common bonds that exist for the Ummah.

Jonathan Raban, writing in the *Guardian* of April 19th 2003, eloquently and passionately describes the working of the Ummah in the context of Iraq where he attempts to explain why the international body of believers has been so vitalised by its own pain and rage. In his explanation, the idea of the body is central. On the website of *Khilafah.com*, a London-based magazine, Yusuf Patel writes: 'The Islamic Ummah is manifesting her deep feeling for a part of her body, which is in the process of being severed'. Raban argues that 'it would be a great mistake to read this as mere metaphor or rhetorical flourish. Ummah is sometimes defined as the community, sometimes the nation, sometimes the body of Muslim believers around the globe, and it has a physical reality, without parallel in any other religion' (*Guardian*, 2003; Zaman, 2002).

The belief that unites

That is not to say that all Muslims are devout and that all Muslims think alike. Given the insecurities and divisions that exist within the Islamic world, within the UK, in Europe and elsewhere, that would be nonsense. Islam is, however, a broad mosque. It is true to say that there is more that unites Muslims than divides them. Regardless of doctrinal differences, all Muslims share the core belief that 'There is none worthy of worship but God, and Muhammad is God's Messenger' (the *Shahadah*). This faith is the first and most important element of Muslim identity. Closely linked to faith is the fundamental dimension of spirituality, which is the way in which the believer keeps alive, intensifies and strengthens faith. In Islamic terms, spirituality is about remembering God, about reciting His names and observing the prayers and other rituals as a way to remember (the *dhikr*). Crucially, it has also developed a socio-political dimension in terms of establishing and maintaining justice and piety in social institutions.

Faith has to be lived to be real. The Prophet (pbuh) lived his faith and taught his faith on a daily basis. He constantly demonstrated that love, bounty, generosity and justice were the true values and repeated to his Companions that they should be good to one another, respect all living beings, nature and, most importantly of all, treat with equity all Muslims or non-Muslims, men or women, young or old. The Prophet stressed the importance of family values, of kindness and of tolerance.

There is a real need for teachers and local government officers to understand the Muslim Frame of Reference and to use it to help their pupils understand and deal with the issues that preoccupy many European Muslims. That frame of reference has two major foundations: the *Qur'an*, – the divine revelation that was given to the Prophet Muhammad over a 23-year period; and *the Sunnah*. The *Sunnah* are the traditions and practices of Muhammad and the first generation of Muslims, which include the *Hadith* – the collections of the Messenger's reported sayings. In addition, generations of scholars, known as *ulama*, have sought to interpret texts and to agree upon interpretations through *ijma* (consensus) and *iyas* (analogy). These four sources provide the canonical basis for Muslim belief and practice.

For many Muslims in Europe, Islam is the key determinant in their lives. Yet schools are not always sensitive to this. Pupils, as they enter through the school portals, are required to leave their religion at home, not through design but because so often the school, as a secular institution, is simply unaware of the centrality of Islam in the life of its Muslim pupils. There is a great and understandable reluctance to begin to debate what it means to be a European Muslim. Some Muslims would disagree with the concept altogether and argue that they are Muslims in Europe, presumably looking to a better place to practise their religion, 'whose hearts and minds are overseas'. Similarly, many teachers do not feel equipped to help steer their pupils through the complicated Islamic minefield. Both groups are perhaps fearful lest they open an Islamic Pandora's box and unleash forces they would be unable to control. But such are the forces, pressures and influences on young Muslims that schools must grasp the nettle and engage in open and honest dialogue about what it means to be a European Muslim. The discourse must be one between equals, not a discourse that assumes one set of values is superior to another.

Islam and democracy

Debates about the nature of Islam and its place in the West are not, of course, confined to youths. They are reflected at a geopolitical level and resonate in comments and actions made by President Bush and Prime Minister Blair, who continually stress that their war is a war on terror, and not a war on a great religion. For some, recent terrorist events have born out their interpretation of Samuel Huntington's thesis outlined in the *Clash of Civilisations,* where Islam was identified as one of the threats to Western hegemony. Huntington's interpretation of Islam, it should be added, was strongly challenged at the time by many Islamic scholars. The seeming clash of cultures between Muslim values and Western values has been the subject of fierce debate, a debate that goes to the very heart of Muslims and democracy.

Tariq Ramadan, in his comprehensive work, *To be a European Muslim – a study of Islamic sources in the European context* (1999), seeks to answer some of the basic questions about European Muslims' social, political, cultural and legal integration. Drawing upon a thorough knowledge of Islamic sources, he demonstrates that it is possible to lead life as a practising Muslim while living together in multifaith, pluralistic European nation states. The situation in which Muslims find themselves in Europe – a situation that is a direct legacy of European economic and geographic imperialism – has obliged many of them to think deeply about the implications of their faith and its daily practice. This in turn has led to the reopening of questions that Muslim scholars and thinkers had faced at the height of Muslim civilisation a thousand years ago, and have always troubled Muslims living outside Muslim countries. Ironically, those living on the margins of the Muslim world have perforce returned to the theological centre to seek answers. Increasingly, Muslim youths are asking fundamental questions about the place of Islam in Europe and in the world, and seek to know more about Muslim civilisation and its legacy.

First generation immigrants, in a strange and hostile environment and often with a very limited knowledge of Islam, tried to conserve what they saw as essential Islamic values in a land which appeared to them as often permissive, if not promiscuous, in its values. Many clung more to *cultural Islam,* that is, to the particular practices, customs and faith interpretations which had more to do with their own country of origin than with essential doctrine. As Ramadan (1999) argues, one finds the scars of this attitude among younger generations which can manifest themselves in 'self assertion', very often linked with a total oblivion of one's origins and attempts to remain faithful to Islamic references as translated both in thinking and in action, by reaction, rejection, refusal and sometimes aggression.

For some youths the measure of their faith is proportionate to their rejection of the West, as if they defined Islam by what it is not, rather than what it is. They can reduce their religion to a series of prescriptions and rules, to listing what is permitted and lawful (halal) and unlawful (haram). Their own search for Islamic truth is often hampered by their limited knowledge of Arabic and by a lack of understanding of the Qur'an and the *Hadith* that they are encouraged to recite but not generally encouraged to interpret.

In addition, Ramadan maintains that many Muslims have internalised the negative perceptions of themselves as 'the problem': 'It is as if ... they have been colonised by the idea, the *obvious* fact, the *indisputable* evidence that Islam *is* a problem in the West and that Muslims *have* problems with progress, democracy and modernity' (p. 22). On the positive side, there is an increasing tendency for young Muslims to assert their faith identity, but this is counterbalanced by a feeling that they are unable to contribute to the Western Muslim debate and seek their answers from interpretations of the Qur'an, *Hadith* and the subsequent exegetical canons of Islamic law and jurisprudence (the *Fiqh*) that over time have been made by generations of learned Muslim scholars, known collectively as the *ulama*. 'We are witnessing, among young European Muslims, the unhealthy development of a complex whereby they discredit themselves and think that the right responses should come from abroad, from great '*ulama*' residing in Islamic countries'.

Ramadan's technical though highly readable book outlines in some detail the essential values and teachings of Islam and Islamic Sciences. His essential argument is that it is within the tradition for Muslims to discuss how to adapt and adopt their faith to different circumstances, to the vicissitudes of changing times, provided the essentials of the faith are retained. In Islam there is great respect for tradition, and for scholarly knowledge. The absolute nature of the core principles is not open to debate, but this is balanced against the need to interpret those principles in the local contemporary context. Indeed it is God's will that religious diversity exists and to each people he gave a specific message:

> Unto every one of you have We appointed a different law and way of life. And if God had so willed, He could have surely have made you all one single community: but (He willed it otherwise) in order to test you by means of what he vouchsafed unto you. Vie, then with one another in doing good works.

Soon after the Prophet's flight from Makkah to Madinah the Prophet, after consultation with various groups in the region, drew up a document called the *Sahifah*, which has been described as the first written constitution in the world. This constitution legalised a pluralist, multiracial, multicultural society comprising Jews and Muslims. All sectors of the community had the freedom to practise their religion, to earn a living as they saw fit and all were bound by a series of obligations and responsibilities. It was a physical embodiment of Islamic ideals of justice and democracy and laid the foundations of the tolerance that characterised much of the period of Muslim hegemony (Muslim Council of Britain, 2002).

On the face of it, much of this discourse may appear to be esoteric, but issues of citizenship and how we promote it go to the very heart of how we as a nation see ourselves, of how we as educators promote citizenship, and how Muslims perceive education.

The Muslim view of learning/knowledge

... Education should ... cater for the
Growth of 'man' in all its aspects:
Spiritual, intellectual, imaginative,
Physical, scientific, linguistic, both
Individually and collectively and motivate
All these aspects towards goodness and the
Attainment of perfection
(Al-Attar 1979 – from the First World conference on Muslim
Education, Mecca, 1977)

Unsurprisingly, such a view is in accordance with how non-Muslims see education, especially as the term Man in the Qur'an has been interpreted as non-gendered, referring to both men and women when used collectively. It is probably true, however, that most non-Muslims are unlikely to write about the drive to goodness and the attainment of perfection, even though this may be implicit in the values of Western education systems. That emphasis is the essential difference, not that Muslim education negates or denies that which we see as traditionally Western, rather that its overarching goal is attuned to faith in action which in its turn continually leads Muslims to remember God. For Muslims, the ultimate goal is to seek God through Knowledge (*ilm*). Kaye Haw, in *Educating Muslim Girls (1998),* neatly encapsulates the Islamic difference between 'Revealed knowledge' and 'acquired knowledge.' Revealed knowledge is part of the absolute knowledge that is of God and is granted to only a few. For Muslims, the last revelation was to Mohammed (PBUH) himself when Archangel Gabriel delivered the Qur'an to him over a 23-year period. Much of Islamic scholarship is dedicated to interpretations of this revelation. Acquired knowledge on the other hand relates to social, natural and applied sciences but must be firmly placed within the context of revelation

Traditionally, Islam has insisted that reason and revelations are the two drivers in life's quest and in order to reach one's destination both have to be pursued. To put it another way, the search for knowledge can be seen as an act of piety, as equivalent to prayer. The ultimate use of the intellect is the cultivation of the divine attributes, and the role of knowledge in the religo-political life of the *ummah* is decisive and all pervading. It ennobles, enriches and solidifies faith and belief in the revealed word of Allah. All Muslims, theoretically, are under a religious obligation to accept learning as a continuous process in life, and early Muslims were encouraged to use independent judgement based on the righteous intention to overcome the difficulties of life. It was due to the insistence on research and enquiry as a religious duty that early Muslims produced some of the first and greatest scientific works and developed a great civilisation. Without this scientific knowledge, many of the religious duties and ceremonies would not have been possible, as so much of it is based on intricate calculations of the lunar calendar and many of the complex laws of Islam required considerable knowledge of diverse sciences. Without careful scholarship, much of it comparative, Muslim scholars could not fulfil their duty to God.

The Importance of Islamic civilisation and its place in the mainstream curriculum

It is probably a truism that for their own sense of self-esteem and worth all pupils need to see themselves reflected positively in the curriculum of the schools they attend. The DfES funded CREAM project was designed to discover the extent to which the experience of Muslim pupils could be used by mainstream schools in the National Curriculum. The research team trawled the national curriculum and its schemes of work from early years to 16 plus and wrote to over 50 LEAs that had significant numbers of Muslim pupils. They found that although there were many curricular areas that had the potential to reflect these experiences, there was little, with the exception of Religious Education and Citizenship, with which Muslims could identify (DfES, 2004). Many pupils could go through most, if not all, their educational career without coming into contact with the wealth and legacies of the great age of Islamic civilisation. In its first thousand years, Islamic civilisation flourished from Spain to Central Asia. While Europe suffered what has been called the Dark Ages, Muslims translated, enhanced and developed much of the thinking of the ancient Greeks and made remarkable contributions in the realms of science, medicine, art and architecture, literature and astrology. Many of the greatest Sufi mystical tracts and poetry were also written during this period.

Many of these great achievements are succinctly documented in Bloom and Blair's book, *Islam Empire of Faith*, which was written to accompany the BBC2 series in 2001. Bloom and Blair, however, steer clear of any attempt to assess Islam's contribution to the modern world. Increasingly, Islamic scholars are taking up this challenge and are cogently arguing that the roots of the modern world with its emphasis on liberty and freedom, science and technology, owes much to Muslim scholarship and research. Professor Salim T.S. Hassani, of the Foundation for Technology and Science (in www.Muslimheritage.com) takes up what is now becoming a key theme: *One Thousand Years of Missing History*. He argues that European historians have generally ignored the link between the ancient Greeks, Islamic civilisation and the European renaissance and enlightenment. Europe owes a great debt to the Muslim scholars who translated key texts from the Greeks, who developed medicine, founded the first universities and were responsible for a great flowering of intellectual thought. Hassani's article ends with an extract from a speech on the treasures of Islam from the Belgian minister of culture, delivered in Antwerp in March 2003:

> These Islamic values that are reflected by the great Islamic civilisation have contributed to the progress and development of our Western society. Knowledge is clearly the key to development. Thanks to the knowledge and the intellect of the Muslim scientist we were able to benefit from mathematics, anatomy, chemistry, philosophy, astronomy...In other words, thanks to Islam, knowledge was preserved, further developed and passed on and this is without any doubt one of the important treasures of Islam.

Towards a 'new' strategy

Fifteen major reasons why education systems must move towards a new strategy that deals with Muslims in education have been outlined above. Perhaps the adjective 'new' is a misnomer, as it is unlikely that the education system ever had an old one. The rationale, however, is clear: if Faith is the key determinant of Muslim pupils' lives and identities, and if the key vehicle for accessing faith is revealed and acquired knowledge, then it follows that education systems, schools, LEAs, their many agencies and partners, and Further and Higher Education Institutions must take steps to understand more deeply the key components and issues for Muslim pupils. This deeper understanding must lead to effective strategies and real action in all areas of educational life, so that both Muslims and non-Muslims can begin to understand the contribution of Islam to our shared histories and the major issues that face British Muslims today, in terms of the local, national and international contexts. National and local government departments, Health Authorities, LEAs, and schools (mainstream, independent and complementary) must engage in a robust dialogue that leads to the formulation of a new strategy.

This dialogue will have slightly different dimensions in the various countries and contexts that make up Europe, for each nation state has its own unique education system. The underlying principles and processes are, however, common to them all.

There are fifteen key component parts, listed below, of this strategy for national and local government, for LEAs and HEIs, for schools and all their partners. There are no easy answers and quick fixes to issues that have their roots deep in our shared histories and narratives. The keys are mutual understanding and dialogue. The development and implementation of a new strategy and the weighting given to its components will vary from institution to institution and from country to country, but certain generic actions are applicable in various degrees to everybody. All those involved with education, therefore, should:

1. **Seek and empathise with** a greater understanding that goes beyond the daily practices and rules of Islam to an awareness of the centrality of the love and remembrance of God in Islam, and of the major issues faced by (European) Muslim pupils, their parents and their communities.

2. **Map** current practices and expertise that relate to meeting the needs of Muslim pupils and tackling Islamophobia.

3. **Discover and disseminate** the good practice that already exists in many of our schools and institutions, and on the many websites dedicated to Islamic issues.

4. **Devise** strategies that are dedicated to closing the achievement/attainment gap and raising the self esteem of Muslims as Muslims.

5. **Build** these strategies into all major plans.

6. **Draw up** and implement an overarching strategy, 'Islam and Education,' that relates to all departments.

7. **Ensure** that all race equality policies address meeting the needs of Muslim pupils and countering Islamophobia.

8. **Insist** that all providers of Professional Development build the Islamic perspective into their courses, conferences, coaching and mentoring wherever applicable.

9. **Support and help develop** the complementary sector and **build** effective links with mainstream schools.

10. **Support and help** schools to provide consistent and coherent support to help their Muslim pupils grow up as 'good Muslims'.

11. **Use** Islamic values such as justice, compassion and service and the Islamic view of learning to motivate students.

12. **Use** the unique contributions that Islam has made to learning to raise students' self esteem.

13. **Encourage** the development of curriculum materials and perspectives that reflect Muslim contributions to the contemporary world.

14. **Encourage** Muslims in their debate about what it means to be a European Muslim.

15. **Help build** the capacity of young Muslims to articulate and develop their own discourse, frame of reference and solutions.

Some organisations, either singly or collectively, may wish to appoint an individual or individuals with specific responsibility for Muslim affairs. Others will seek to fit it in with existing responsibilities. Some will seek funding from external sources to support the development and implementation of such a strategy. Others may use existing funds. Either way, the strategy will need to be monitored and evaluated as part of the normal institutional arrangements. There are some key process points, however, that all involved organisations would do well to consider.

Recommended processes that underpin the development, implementation and evaluation of a new strategic approach

This is a dialogical and dialectical process. And it is a two way process that encourages Muslims and non-Muslims to question, to become reflective, to examine Muslim views of the education service as it stands. Similarly, it encourages education services to examine their own attitudes to Islam. There are no easy answers; no straightforward one-size-fits-all. It will not be a comfortable or easy journey and many of the questions and challenges will emerge as the process develops.

The basic principles succinctly outlined by Michael Fullan (2001) in *Leading in a Culture of Change* perfectly cohere with the strategic analysis. He could be describing 'Islam and education' when he writes that, 'the big problems of the day are complex, rife with paradoxes and dilemmas. For these problems there are no once-and-for-all answers. Yet we expect our leaders to provide solutions.' The five components of leadership that Fullan identifies resonate with my arguments here. He maintains that:

- Leaders must act with *moral purpose*, with the intention of making a positive difference to the lives of customers (pupils) and of society; and that moral purpose is normally accompanied by a sense of urgency

- Leaders must understand the *change process*

- *Relationships, relationships relationships* are the essential prerequisite for all effective change, and we need to pay as much attention to how we treat people – the pupils, the parents, and the communities – as we typically pay to structures, strategies and statistics

- *Knowledge creation and sharing* – turning information into knowledge is a social process, and for that you need good relationships

- *Coherence making* is a key leadership function but the nature of leadership must change. For Fullan, 'the leader becomes a context setter, the designer of a learning experience – not an authority figure with solutions' (p.112)

This essentially means that we must engage in open non-prejudicial discourse with the complete range of interested parties, including Heads, Directors and local government officers acting in partnership as the context setters. This would mean that we proactively involve

- Muslim Communities
- parents and governors
- Madrassas and mosques
- pupils, Youth Voices/Student Councils
- Community Cohesion/youth workers
- Higher and Further Education Institutions

In conclusion

One could be forgiven for thinking that this new strategic approach is too large, too complex and too fraught with problems to begin even to contemplate. It is a daunting challenge. Failure to accept that challenge will, however, lead to more problems for the Muslim communities themselves, and to an inevitable increase in Islamophobia, as the roots of prejudice and discrimination will not be tackled. For Muslims and non-Muslims alike however, there is no better way to end than with the words that form the Prophet Mohammed's final sermon, words that underpin the essence of our new strategy:

> People, verily your Lord and Sustainer is one
> and your ancestor is one. All of you descend
> from Adam and Adam was made of earth.
> There is no superiority for an Arab over a
> non-Arab nor for a non-Arab over an Arab;
> neither a white man over a black man nor a
> black man over a white man except the superiority
> gained through God consciousness. Indeed the
> noblest of you is the one who is most deeply
> conscious of God.
> (*From the farewell sermon of the noble Prophet, delivered in Arafat and Mina in the month of Dhu'l-Hijjah 10 AH/630 CE*)

9

Educational Choices for Immigrant Muslim Communities: secular or religious?

Irene Donohoue Clyne

Introduction

One of the most significant changes in the Australian educational landscape in the past twenty years has been the rapid expansion of new non-government schools, facilitated in part by changes to Federal Government funding policies for new schools introduced in 1997 (DEETYA, 1997), which have made it easier for community and religious organisations to establish new schools. These schools represent the whole spectrum of non-government education, from the well established elite schools and the Catholic education system to small parent-controlled Christian schools, under-resourced Aboriginal community schools and 27 Islamic schools. Current government rhetoric on parental choice and its own electoral interests, together with increased funding, have underpinned this expansion.

But this growth of new private schools and the perceived inequalities in funding have led to some resentment within the wider community. In the past two years, newspapers have tapped into this resentment by running numerous public interest articles on religious schools with headlines such as 'Islam leads in rush to faith education' (Morris, www.smh.com.au/text/articles/2003/06 /22/1056220477178.htm) and 'Funding Favours Islamic Schools' (Maiden, www.theaustralian.com.au/printpage/0,5942/8352556. 00.html). These give a false impression of the growth in Islamic schools and also about their comparative funding. Since the government funding formula is based on a socio-economic index, Islamic schools generally receive higher per capita funding than schools in wealthy areas, but they do not have the same capacity to generate income through fees. An independent school may charge fees of $15,000 per year whilst Islamic and other low fee schools charge between $750-$2000 per year.

Australians have an ambivalent attitude towards the non-government or private education sector and funding decisions are always very political. On the one hand, there is a commitment to an inclusive and democratic government education system usually described as free, secular and compulsory, which reflects the socio-cultural diversity of our society and, on the other hand, many parents believe that non-government schools, most of which have been established by religious organisations, are better resourced, have higher standards of discipline and better educational outcomes. Until comparatively recently, deciding which school would provide an appropriate education for their children, secular or religious, has been problematic for Muslim parents, since their only realistic option was a government school. But the separation of religion and education exemplified in the Australian dual education system has created an ideological problem, for Islam is an all embracing religion, incorporating not only personal beliefs but all dimensions of the community. Pulcini's study (1990), examining the conflict between traditional Islamic and American values in education, identified the separation of religion and state as a crucial issue for Muslim parents seeking to educate their children. Parents believe that:

> the public education system ensures the separation of church and state, a pivotal element of the American way of life. To those from Islamic cultures, such a separation is perplexing at best and unthinkable at worst. In an education system, this separation is seen as having a number of deleterious effects. (Pulcini, 1990:128)

Like other immigrant religious communities, Muslims have begun to resolve this question of choice by establishing schools to provide a religious context for teaching and learning and developing an Islamic identity.

The struggle for Al Noori

This chapter examines the social and educational context of the choices Muslim parents in Australia make about the education of their children. In begins with the story of Al Noori Muslim Primary School, which was the first Islamic school established in Australia. The story of Al Noori is a metaphor for the struggle of Muslims to educate their children in Australia: a struggle against ignorance and prejudice within the community; the obstructionist tactics of local government officials; the lack of financial and educational resources; and inexperience in establishing a school. The existence of this small Muslim primary school in the Western suburbs of Sydney, is due to the extraordinary vision, persistence and religious commitment of Siddiq Buckley and Silma Ihram (formerly Buckley), who were converts to Islam. The story of Al Noori is significant because nearly all the Islamic schools opened since 1983 have benefited from the experiences of Al Noori. However, as immigrant Muslim communities in other countries have also found (Dwyer and Meyer, 1996), every school opened has met some opposition. As converts to Islam rather than immigrants to Australia, Silma and Siddiq had insiders' knowledge of the education system but were outsiders to the traditional Muslim organisations. They recognised that neither private Christian nor government schools would be able to provide an Islamically acceptable education for their children. So as Silma explained in her book, they decided to start their own school (Buckley, 1991).

They received little support from Muslim community organisations and this created a problem of credibility in the media and made their struggle even harder. Siddiq (1987: 25) identified the Muslim community itself as a stumbling block... 'internally factionalised, ethnically diverse, politically impotent, intellectually moribund'. Even today, the ethnic and sectarian divisions within the Muslim community have prevented a coherent policy on establishing Islamic schools. The Buckleys did not have easy access to overseas Islamic charities to provide capital funding and they struggled financially to equip their school. Yet individual parents recognised this initiative as very important, with one mother offering to sell her house rather than let the school close down (Cross, 1983).

Siddiq and Silma's status as converts to Islam added another dimension to their struggle to establish an Islamic school because, as Siddiq noted, 'being Muslim reverts, we have no Muslim community of our own kind for support and assistance. We are strangers in a strange land, strengthened only by our faith in Islam' (Buckley, 1987:24-25). An official Muslim community spokesperson could have mobilised the Muslim community to provide more than moral support, but these Australian converts were seen as in competition with the official umbrella organisation, Australian Federation of Islamic Councils (AFIC), which was intending to use overseas charitable donations to build a school. In 1988 AFIC eventually established Malek Fahd Islamic College.

Finding a suitable site for Al Noori and gaining local government approval for its use was a problem. The strength of opposition from the local community to the proposed Muslim school was unexpected, with racism and rumours of PLO involvement virtually ensuring that the local government council would not register their premises for use as a school. Siddiq noted in an interview (Donohoue Clyne, 2000: 162) that anti-Muslim lobby groups 'perpetuated the myth in the local community's eyes that we were foreigners who had come here and were imposing ourselves'. Their application to register premises as a school was rejected by the local government authorities on the grounds that such a school would lead to 'splintering of the education system and segregation of children from the mainstream of the community' (Buckley, 1987: 25), even though these reasons exceeded the authority of local government. The official reasons cited for rejecting proposed school sites, however, were generally about the insufficient amenities of the proposed school building or the effect such a school would have on the amenity of the area, rather than about community based concerns (Buckley, 1987).

Control over technical details such as drainage problems or parking requirements gave local governments enormous power to interfere with the educational needs of the Muslim community. The application of this power was Islamophobia dressed up as environmental concerns. Only when school premises had been approved by local government authorities could the new school be registered with the Education Department and registration was a pre-requisite for both Commonwealth and State government funding. Registration is a complex process requiring extensive documentation of curriculum content, pedagogy, school organisation, staff qualifications and experience as well as a suitable site. The long and costly struggle to find premises that could be certified as suitable for a school lasted six years (Buckley, 1991).

Al Noori and the wider community

Embedded in the struggle to establish Al Noori Muslim Primary School are a number of important issues. Firstly, the perception of Muslims as outsiders shaped the response of the authorities to their application to establish a new school. Despite the existence of a dual education system with well-established non-government schools reflecting the religious traditions of many different Christian and Jewish denominations, this was the first application from Muslims for a school of their own. Their application generated a surprising amount of opposition, considering that it met the guidelines of the existing New Schools Policy, especially those relating to a sustainable enrolment pattern. Shboul (1984:18) attributed this type of reaction to the challenges of an unfamiliar religious and cultural tradition, since there had been little engagement with Muslims in the educational context.

But in addition, the discourse relating to the founders of Al Noori and their intentions reflects a fear of the outsider and of behaviours such as wearing modest Islamic dress or fasting during Ramadan, which were seen as alien. This has unfortunately been a continuing discourse. Concern was expressed that an Islamic school (the preferred description of the Muslim community) would create some kind of educational ghetto, separating children from mainstream Australian society. Recent comments by a professor of education (Burke, 2003) warned that, 'the growth of religious-based schools could contribute to a Balkanisation of Australian society', while the president of a Parents and Citizens association commented 'We truly believe segregation takes away the opportunity to know your neighbour ... excluding and dividing is a very dangerous way to go'.

Opposition to the idea of government funding for non-government schools, especially religious schools, has been very much part of the rhetoric of Australian education. When the decision to provide federal funding to non-government schools was made in 1969, parent associations and teacher unions argued that religious schools would divide our multicultural nation into 'ethnic and religious ghettos' (Mortensen, 1985: 223). The Muslim community was not part of this debate but like other immigrant groups it has been affected by this decision. The strong and ongoing opposition to the principle of state aid (government funding) to religious schools is summarised by Maslen (1982: 275): 'if religious or other groups want to run their own schools, well and good, although the state should not subsidise them to do so.' In the 1960s it was Catholic schools that were to be feared; in 2004 it is Islamic schools.

Al Noori school supporters campaigned using the slogan 'Good Muslims make good Australians' (Buckley, 1991:15). In an interview in 1991, Siddiq described their attempts to be friendly and open with the school's neighbours, repairing roofs after a storm and inviting them to afternoon tea (Donohoue Clyne, 2000:163). However, it was not until an incident during the Gulf War of 1990 that the school was accepted by the local community. The children of Al Noori School wrote directly to President Saddam Hussein to plead the case of Australian hostages in Kuwait, including the grandson of the school's neighbour. 'It was probably the first instance ever in Australia that Muslims were portrayed as both patriotically Australian and genuinely Muslim at the same time' (Buckley, 1997: 3). This gesture received positive media and community support. It was also an important educative experience for the children of Al Noori School.

The school's mission statement made clear that its students, secure in their commitment to Islam, were part of the broader multicultural Australian community. Developing an Australian-Muslim identity, from the diversity of national backgrounds which make up the Australian Muslim community has become an aim of many Islamic Schools. This is generally expressed in their information brochures, for example, 'the aim of the school is to foster a new generation of Muslims who are proud to be Australian' (Werribee Islamic College) or on their websites 'to produce Muslim graduates who are proud to be Australian Muslims' (Minaret College). This commitment to Australia is an important marketing feature of Islamic schools, since the wider community sometimes views them with suspicion.

A recent incident illustrates the challenges Islamic schools continually face to gain acceptance by the wider community. In March 2003, the Federal Minister of Education wrote to state ministers of education asking them to ensure that Islamic schools were 'meeting curriculum requirements and not encouraging anti-Christian and anti-Western sentiment among their students' (Guerrera and Jackson, 2003:4). His letter was made public when the state Minister for Education, Anna Bligh, tabled it in the Queensland Parliament. Subsequently the matter was reported widely in the national media, with the Premier of Queensland, Peter Beatty, quoted in news bulletins as saying 'this week they are picking on Islamic schools, next week it could be Catholic schools', unconsciously evoking memories of earlier bitter sectarian debates on government funding for religious schools. The minister justified his action on the basis that the opinions of concerned citizens had led to his letter, although no actual evidence of a violation of funding guidelines was revealed. In a climate of heightened community awareness due to international acts of terrorism, such comments were threatening to the Muslim community. Politics aside, the Minister's action seemed to indicate a lack of knowledge of the rather stringent state government requirements with which all new non-government schools must comply to receive registration and hence funding, but also a belief that Islamic schools are in some way un-Australian.

This notion gives a thin veneer of legitimacy to the actions of those involved in anti-Muslim graffiti, theft or destruction of school property. Baldock (1991) noted that during the first Gulf War, identifiably Islamic buildings including schools were vandalised and that with each international act of terrorism that is linked to Muslims, Islamic schools and their students are vulnerable to local acts of terrorism. Islamic schools face the continual challenge of re-assuring their students that Islamic law does not condone terrorism but that as students at an identifiable Islamic school they need to take responsibility for the way the broader community sees Islam (Karvelas, http://www.theaustralian.news.com.au). By identifying Islamic schools as potentially anti-Christian and anti-Western, the Federal Minister of Education is linking these schools, and the communities they serve, with terrorism. As Hippler and Lueg (1995) suggest:

> We invent an Islam that suits us, that best fulfils our politico-psychological needs. This is exactly how we arrive at a clean separation between 'us' and 'them' (the Other), between inside and outside that are never supposed to meet and thus we succeed in fencing off and fortifying our own Western identity.

Attacks upon the integrity of Islamic schools are not limited to politicians. In the current discourse about Islamic schools are themes of separation from the mainstream society and un-Australian values and beliefs. For example, a report entitled *Immigration and Schooling in the 1990s* (Cahill et al., 1996:92) recorded a number of negative concerns about some full-time ethno-religious schools, which included, 'The pervading ethno-centricity of the leadership group, combined with a lack of student contact with other types of Australian students, and historically dubious curriculum materials emanating from the source country.'

These unsubstantiated comments were interpreted as referring to Islamic schools, although not one Islamic school was included in the Cahill study. But the report generated ill-informed media coverage which implied that Islamic schools would cause social division and legitimise discrimination against girls because they were required to wear the hijab and that this was unacceptable to Australians (Donohoue Clyne, 1997a: A11). Melbourne daily newspapers presented images of young hijab-wearing girls sitting at the back of the classroom, as evidence of gender based discrimination, while the subtle non-verbal communication of the hijab and its religious meaning were interpreted through Western cultural values. Wearers of hijab themselves were thus discriminated against and devalued (Donohoue Clyne, 2003a).

Culturally appropriate education

A second important issue evident in the story of Al Noori is the perceived absence of culturally appropriate education in both government and private schools. The catalyst for Silma and Siddiq's decision to establish their own Muslim school was their belief that only a Muslim school would be able to provide a quality education in an environment that would respect each child's Muslim identity. This belief is consistent with those expressed by Durkee (1987), who was involved in establishing an Islamic community school in the USA and those of Yusef Islam, who established Islamia School in the UK (Hulmes, 1989:28). All are reverts to Islam, educated in the education systems they now reject. A 'God-centred curriculum' in which religious beliefs shape and permeate the curriculum has been identified (Al Attas, 1979; Halstead, 1986a) as an important reason for establishing a religious school.

This is certainly the case for the rapid growth of low fee Christian schools. The Australian government education system, although secular, is underpinned by values derived from Judeo-Christian traditions, which have permeated the core of the school curriculum and pedagogy. Although these are not necessarily in conflict with Islamic teaching, there is limited provision within the curriculum for specific religious instruction, although schools with Muslim students are usually sympathetic to religious practices such as prayer, fasting or Islamic dress. The discrimination against overt religious symbols such as the French government is implementing would be totally unacceptable in Australia. When Muslim community members were asked what kind of education they wanted for their children (Donohoue Clyne, 2001:119) they chose an education which is infused with religious teaching and practice in all areas of the curriculum and of life. As a parent explained,

What Muslim children need most in their Islamic education is an education that encompasses all aspects of life with qualified teachers. It is not only important teaching the Arabic language and memorising the holy Qur'an, but children need to be taught how to become good citizens and how to form families united in solidarity.

School curricula, however, tend to be Eurocentric, ignoring the contributions of Muslims to world knowledge and even the contribution of Muslims to the growth of multicultural Australia. When asked why they would choose an Islamic school for their children, over 60 per cent of Muslim community members mentioned the teaching of the Qur'an, a curriculum which reflected Islamic values and a Muslim environment in the school as most important (Donohoue Clyne 2001, 2003b). So Muslim parents who want their children to learn about Islamic culture and history need to look outside of state provision.

Teaching styles in Australian schools tend to encourage an individualistic and independent approach to learning, which often questions authority and is future orientated (Hofstede, 1986). This contrasts with the collectivist approach to learning and acceptance of traditional knowledge and authority preferred by many immigrant Muslim parents (Donohoue Clyne, 1998). Parents interviewed by this writer expressed fear that a secular school would undermine their children's religious commitment and expose them to un-Islamic practices. As a Somali parent explained, 'parents are panicking because they are frightened their children are being swept away into alien activities such as smoking, drugs or sexual relations' (Donohoue Clyne, 2001:124). Parents believe that weak discipline in Western schools and lack of authority on the part of teachers serve to undermine their own control over their children. Discipline, respect and control are culturally determined but treated differently in Australian schools and immigrant Muslim parents are often disturbed by actions or regulations which they perceive as undermining their authority. A similar attitude was evident in von Hirsch's research among Muslims in Sweden. She quotes a Muslim father,

God placed the responsibility of children in the hands of parents and we as parents know what is best for our children. How can

> strangers in public offices know what is best for my child? If we
> punish our children it is out of love. Even the Koran says one is
> permitted to slap the child (von Hirsch, 1996: 87).

The potential conflict of values between parents' expectation of
schools and classroom practice is a recurrent theme in immigrant
Muslim parents' discourse about education (Berns McGown,
1999:106; Donohoue Clyne, 2001:122-124). Such parents expect
schools to create a learning environment that teaches Islam and
affirms Muslim practice but this does not happen in government
schools.

Choosing a religious or secular education

The question of choice is another important issue highlighted by
the Al Noori story. Siddiq and Silma chose a religious education
rather than a secular one, although they had to struggle to make
this choice possible. The choice is not possible for all Muslim
parents because many do not have access to such a school for
financial or geographical reasons. Currently, 90 per cent of
Muslim children attend government schools, so are receiving a
secular education. Cultural and religious diversity creates a challenge to existing curricula and pedagogy in government, which
still needs to be met. There are also Muslim parents who have
chosen other options to ensure their children are educated in their
religion, such as sending their children to mosque schools held on
the weekends or to Saturday schools where they can improve their
Arabic language skills, or deliberately teach Islam at home.

Some parents interviewed have made enormous sacrifices to enrol
their children in an Islamic school, including one family which
had sold their house in a fairly wealthy suburb to move closer to
an Islamic school. There is considerable support for the idea of
Islamic schools within the Muslim community because of the perceived benefits such schools would bring. For example, over 80
per cent of community members surveyed (Donohoue Clyne,
2000; 2003c) believe Islamic schools would teach Islamic culture,
develop children's Islamic identity, allow children to make friends
with other Muslim children and be taught correct behaviour.
These beliefs are consistent with those of Silma and Siddiq.

Currently there are twenty-seven funded Islamic schools, with at least two or three others currently operating unfunded because they are unable to meet the requirements for registration and hence funding. Australia-wide, Islamic schools educate approximately 10 per cent of school-age Muslim children. Islamic schools have been established in all states except Tasmania and the Northern Territory. Nearly all the Islamic schools cover the full thirteen years of education (kindergarten to year 12) and are co-educational, but classes are single sex at secondary school. This pattern differs markedly from the single-sex secondary schools established by Muslims in the United Kingdom and perhaps reflects the different ethnic composition of the communities in each country.

Islamic schools have been established by dedicated individuals such as Siddiq and Silma Buckley, ethnic community organisations, the Australian Federation of Islamic Councils and private foundations. Overseas charitable trusts have provided seed funding for the establishment of a small number of Islamic schools but ongoing funding is dependent on federal and state government grants plus the comparatively modest fees paid by parents. Although Islamic schools will only ever educate a minority of Australian Muslim children, their existence is a symbol that the Muslim community, in a collective sense, has matured in terms of infrastructure and has the economic and political resources to support its own schools. Muslims are showing commitment to Australia by establishing schools but there is a belief among some parents that private schools provide a certain cachet to a community.

What does the future hold for the education of Muslim children in Australia?

The Al Noori story proves that two pioneers of Islamic education managed to overcome the obstructionist tactics of government officials and opposition within the wider community to claim what was legally theirs, the right to government funding to support a non-government school. Al Noori provides a model of Islamic education for Australian Muslim students. Although many of the Islamic schools are not fully resourced and have yet to achieve their potential, the Muslim community strongly supports them. On a somewhat negative note, those parents who are pro-active in their children's education and have chosen an Islamic school can no longer influence the curriculum in government schools. The presence of Islamic schools gives the Muslim community, although not all parents, the choice between a secular and a religious education. The long term benefit of these schools is expressed in the campaign slogan of Al Noori, 'Good Muslims make Good Australians!' Well-educated Muslims, who understand and practise their religion without the cultural and political attachments that have been so divisive in the community and for Muslims worldwide, should be able to overcome any remnants of Islamophobia in the community.

10

Developing an Appropriate Sexual Health Education Curriculum Framework for Muslim Students

Fida Sanjakdar

Introduction

The school curriculum is generally viewed as all the knowledge and skills schools are accountable for (Marsh and Willis 1999; Saylor *et al.*, 1981) and the school curriculum development process as one that involves the political, cultural and the social climates of the school community (Lovat and Smith, 2003; Walker, 2003; Brady and Kennedy, 1999). As social institutions, schools are subject to considerable pressure from society. The on-going changes in health education agendas in Australian schools suggests that schools are very responsive to such pressure. The history of Australian health education curriculum invariably reflects change in society at large and the way in which society defines the school's purpose.

However, despite the cultural and ethnic diversification of Australia's society, the present health education curriculum decision-making, development and practice exert a dominant Judeo-Christian values system and ideology (Donohoue Clyne, 2001; Lindsay *et al.*, 1987). Australian schools have become agents that incorporate and transmit a 'monocultural' (Halstead and Reiss, 2003) education ideology to a multicultural, multiethnic, multireligious and multilingual society, and the curriculum has become a powerful method of legitimacy, conformity and social control. Although there is a growing Muslim student population in many Australian schools, calls for culturally appropriate health education curriculum, promotion and prevention programmes (Bennett, 1992; Kirk and Tinning, 1990) to address the sexual health needs of Muslim students are largely overlooked. What is still needed and what this chapter seeks to do, is provide a curriculum development and dissemination framework for the teaching of sexual health to Muslim students.

The Islamic position on sexual health

Discussion, teaching and learning about sex, sexuality and sexual health, are not taboo or opposed in Islam. In fact, given the centrality of sexuality in human affairs, in both the public and private spheres, sexuality occupies a prominent place in Islam. Both the Qur'an and the *Hadith* (the sayings and traditions of the Prophet Muhammad, peace be upon him) have placed much emphasis on acquiring knowledge in all areas, and in the days of Prophet Muhammad (pbuh), Muslim men and women were never too shy to ask questions, including those related to private matters such as sexuality.

Rules concerning sexual health govern many Islamic issues such as prayer, (*salat*), fasting (*sawm*), bathing (*ghusl*), marriage (*ziwaj*), divorce (*talaaq*), performing the pilgrimage (*hajj*), as well as the entire spectrum of human needs and behaviour, including kindness, fairness, justice and equality. Education regarding sexual health in Islam is considered part of the religious upbringing of a child (Ashraf, 1998; Mabud, 1998; Noibi, 1998; Sarwar, 1996) and centres around the religious and moral concepts of unity (*tawheed*), trusteeship (*khilafah*) and worship (*ibadah*). An Islamic perspective on the sexual health education curriculum must contain 'Islamicised' knowledge, to which the teaching of the Qur'an and the *Hadith* are central. Curriculum content and pedagogy must be underpinned by Islamic Law (Sharia), which recognises that any prohibitions (e.g. sex outside of marriage or homosexuality) are taken with faith that God has our best interest at heart, guiding us away from potentially destructive behaviour (Al-Qaradawi, 1960). When the Qur'an, the *Hadith* and *Sharia* are combined, an Islamic philosophy of education emerges (see Figure 1), where the acquisition of knowledge (*ilim*) is aimed to develop intellect (*aql*) and nurture the soul (*ruh*), which will lead to the promotion of both social justice (*adl*) and public welfare (*istislah*).

Figure 1: The Islamic philosophy of education

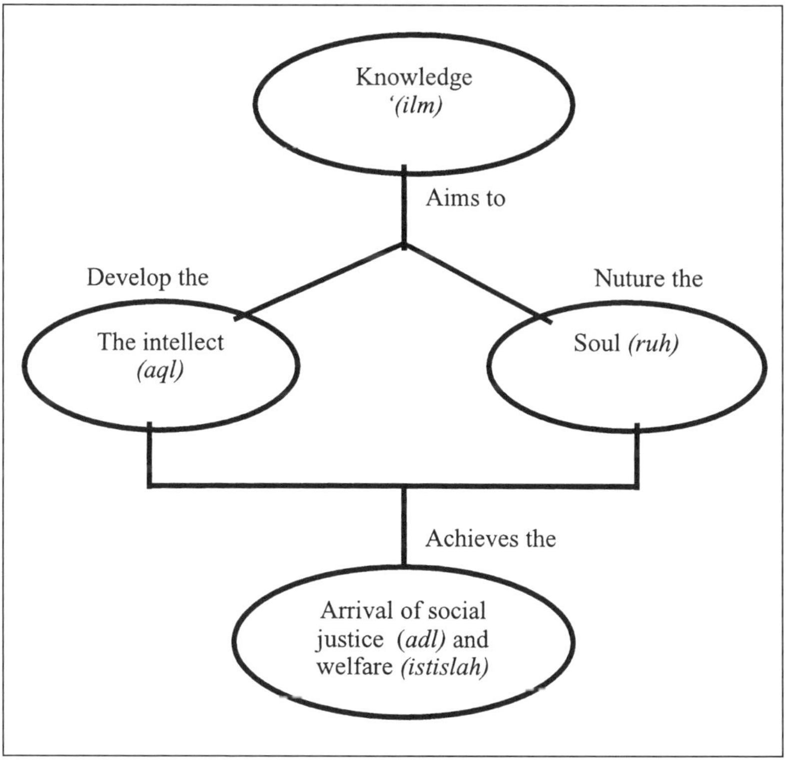

The Islamic position on sexual health education is therefore an avenue for exploring Islamic ideology and establishing Islamic consciousness. Sexual health education becomes a vehicle for spiritual development and hence compulsory for every Muslim.

The sexual health education curriculum in Australian schools

Australia has eight separate government education systems, each with its own curriculum documents, assessment systems and credentialing procedures (Green, 2003). Despite the lack of uniformity in curriculum frameworks and guidelines, Australian schools share the same health education agenda: to advance the health of students (Colquhoun *et al*, 1997; Nutbeam *et al.*; 1993; Lavin *et al.*, 1992). Throughout history, health education in Australian schools has been a school subject heavily influenced by societal changes. Its permeable character has caused many shifts in policy, practice and perspectives.

To counter the rising divorce rate, an increase in venereal diseases and illegitimate births between the World Wars, Australian health education curriculum content shifted from the exclusively physical perspective of health (Brodribb, 1981) to maintaining healthy family relationships and producing changes in health related behaviours. This included studies in all the wider aspects of personal development, including sex education. Australia wide, school health education sought to counter the incidence of certain social problems in the community at the time. In Victoria, the aim to prevent the occurrence of various social problems saw the development of school programmes such as Family Life Education in the 1960s (Wolcott, 1987), the Health and Human Relations Education programme (HHR) in 1982 (Ministry of Education,1980) and the Personal Development Frameworks (Ministry of Education, 1989). In New South Wales, students dealt with 'the possible future' including marriage and parenting (New South Wales Education Department, 1984), whereas in Queensland, the social problems and consequences of sexually transmitted illness (STIs) were of particular focus (Logan, 1980).

Heightened attention to teenage pregnancy, drug and alcohol abuse and the new threat of HIV/AIDS, added impetus to the importance given to sexual health in the overall health education curriculum. Although controversy still surrounds the teaching of sexuality in many schools, with some still most comfortable if 'sex' remains invisible in the school curriculum (Epstein and Johnson,

1998), Australian health education is frequently subject to review and redefinition.

With its on-going research and development, Australia has earned local and international respect for innovation in dealing with complex health issues such as drug education, HIV/AIDS and sexual health. However, the influence of a hegemonic culture which has persisted in Australian education (Partington and McCudden, 1992; Bullivant, 1981), has contributed to delivering inequality in health education for different minority groups (Beckett, 1996). The noble intention for the school curriculum to cater to the rich variety of cultural values and traditions currently in Australian society has yet to be realised (Bennett, 1992; Kirk and Tinning, 1990); a case made clear with the Muslim community. Pallotta-Chiarolli (1996:53) sums this up when she writes that 'although schools are increasingly addressing issues of ethnicity, gender and sexuality, what is still not very apparent is the 'interweaving' of multiples sites and multiple codes of meaning in relation to these categories'. As the next section details, the core curriculum in Australian schools functions to enforce an assimilationist mode where an 'assimilationist mentality' is evident, particularly in the humanities and social sciences (Bullivant, 1981) and in health education. As Lindsay, McEwen and Knight's (1987:1) Australian study confirm, health and physical education appear to be 'purposely designed to serve a social integration function of the Judeo-Christian culture'.

The problems associated with sexual health education for Muslim parents and students

Health education has proven to be the most contentious curriculum subject for many Muslim parents and students. Although the themes of English books and perspectives on History can be just as value laden, no other curriculum subject is accorded such attention in Australia. Three main aspects of contemporary practice in school sexual health education have become legitimate targets for Muslim opposition (Halstead, 1997):

- some sexual health education material offends the Islamic principle of decency and modesty;

- sexual health education tends to present certain behaviours as acceptable which Muslims consider sinful

- sexual health education is perceived as undermining the Islamic concept of family life.

Natural modesty

'Every religion has a distinctive quality and the distinctive quality of Islam is modesty' Hadith Bukhari and Muslim (Kazi, 1992: 120)

In Islam, a human being must be treated as a spiritual and moral being. Therefore, sexual health education for Muslim students cannot be purely physical and deviod of spiritual or moral dimensions. The moral framework in sexual health is a form of protective control and is also closely linked with upholding the honour of the family. The concept of natural modesty (haya) in Islam goes far beyond a specific Islamic dress code, dealing with the entire spectrum of Islamic behaviour, attitude and etiquette. For many Muslim parents and students, it is not necessarily the content of the sexual health education curriculum that is a violation of natural modesty but the presentation of the subject as totally divorced from moral and values education (Al-Romi, 2000). As Abdel-Halim (1989: 15) states, teaching the etiquette of dating as it is currently practised in much of the world violates Islamic principles of chastity.

An Australian study on the potential barriers to learning Personal Development, Health and Physical Education (PDHPE) in New South Wales schools characterised by religious diversity (McInerney *et al*, 2000) found that Muslim students experienced more difficulty engaging in PDHPE related activities than their Catholic peers. Issues of modesty 'such as dress, public display, mixed-sex activities' were of greatest concern (*ibid.*:26). A commonality of experiences in health and physical education classes of Muslim students is mirrored in a few overseas studies. In their study of an English secondary school with a large South Asian Muslim population, Carroll and Hollinshead (1993:65) identify four problem areas as points of conflict between students, parents and Asian communities: PE kit, showers, Ramadan and extra-curricular activities. Wearing the sports uniform embarrassed both the boys and girls and their feelings of guilt and shame were exacerbated when activities were held in public places such as playgrounds and community parks. Communal showers, part of the school's health education programme, caused such problems that some students absented themselves from school.

All discussions with Muslim students about sexuality must be within the context of *haya*, and to preserve this modesty, single sex classes for sexual health programmes are preferred, taught by a teacher of the same sex. Popular classroom practices such as demonstrations on 'how to use a condom correctly' do little to safeguard the modesty of Muslim students. Nor do explicit videos depicting nude people or detailed diagrams of the human form. 'Staring at people of the opposite sex or watching people kissing on TV or in the street' (D'Oyen, 1996:78) are also incompatible with the principle of modesty in Islam.

Behaviour in accordance to Islamic law

Muslim parents look for an education that builds and develops Islamic morals, deeds, character and behaviour (Donohoue Clyne, 2001; Sanjakdar, 2000b). Contemporary sexual health education tends to present certain behaviours which Muslims believe are sinful, as normal or acceptable. 'Free sex', 'safe sex', 'boyfriend/girlfriend relationships', for instance, are terms and concepts devoid of any responsibility and accountability and hence in direct violation of Islamic behaviour and Islamic law (*Sharia*).

In Islam, pre-marital, extra-marital and same sex relationships are forbidden and therefore cannot be advocated or taught as alternative lifestyles or forms of behaviour (Halstead and Lewicka, 1998). Muslims are not permitted to touch, date or have intimate relationships including sexual intercourse outside of an Islamic marriage. Language such as 'spending time together alone', 'getting to know each other', 'feelings can run high but lack of experience with close relationships can lead to many unhappy, disappointing and even bitter experiences', as found in secondary school health texts (Davis and Butler, 1996; Wright, 1992), contravene Islamic principles of decency, modesty, chastity, sexual responsibility and accountability.

The widespread 'choice and preference' model of school sex education (Ulanowsky, 1998), is also unacceptable from a Muslim point of view. Qu'ranic injunctions and *Hadith* make it clear that sexual behaviour is not based entirely on 'personal choice', but must be within God's laws (sura 22 verses 5-7, sura 7 verses 80-81). The philosophy underpinning this idea of individual 'freedom' to judge and the individual 'ability' to judge is a secular one. It stands in opposition to the Islamic, conservative philosophy which takes account of the mind, spirit and emotional aspects of sexuality, as well as acknowledging that in adolescence, physical maturity is rarely accompanied by a matching psychological and emotional maturity.

Australian health educators (and those in other Western nations) must be aware that Muslim students are attempting to live an Islamic life in a non-Islamic country. A spiritual and moral dimension to sexual health education can help Muslim students to better understand themselves and see the relevance of religion to their contemporary lives (Reiss and Mabud, 1998). In a pluralist society such as Australia, Muslim students should not be prevented from learning that non-Muslims may hold sexual values or adopt sexual practices different from their own. As Halstead (1997: 320) argues,

> It is appropriate for education in a pluralist society to encourage Muslim children to adopt an attitude of toleration towards behaviour which, although un-Islamic, is acceptable in the broader society. However, great care must be taken in the classroom so that Muslim students do not confuse *toleration* of difference with *celebration* of difference.

Marriage and the family

Marriage is a sacred institution in Islam and must not be ignored in the sexual health education curriculum for Muslim students. In Islam, marriage gives expression to the divine harmony consisting of the complementarity of men and women. Sexual duality in creation reflects the duality on earth (Ashraf, 1998) and is recognised as one of the great signs Allah has bestowed on humankind.

> *And among His signs is this: He creates for you mates out of your own kind, so that you might incline towards them and He en-*

genders mutual love and compassion between you. (Qur'an, 30:21)

He has created you from a single soul and from that soul He created its mate. (Qur'an, 4:1)

Marriage is viewed as a 'legal sexual means and a shield from immorality' (Sarwar, 1996: 24), a social obligation which forms the basis of an orderly society and the cornerstone of building a family; the basic unit of the Islamic society, the *Umma*. While procreation is an aim, it is not an exclusive aim. Companionship and enjoyment of the spouse, along with avoidance of unlawful or sinful relationships are also major objectives.

The current individualistic perspective to sexual health education prioritises personal autonomy and desire over obligations and commitments to others such as family. To avoid undermining the Islamic position and concept of family life, family values must be kept intact in the sexual health education curriculum. So, as Halstead (1997: 320) points out,

> unmarried cohabitation or same-sex partnerships are in direct opposition to Islamic teaching as are any programmes of sex education which imply to Muslim children that relationships which have some of the features of marriage, such as cohabitation, are just as valid as marriage itself.

Present sexual health education practices clash not only with Muslim parents' and students' morals and values about sexuality but also with their sexual ideology. As McKay (1997:285) explains, 'our perceptions, opinions and moral beliefs are derived from within the confines of the interpretative schema of our ideology. In this respect, ideology defines reality, not vice versa'. Restrictive (abstinence-only) and permissive sexual ideologies compete for influence in shaping sexual health education. However, a permissive sexual ideology which endorses many forms of non-procreative sex including masturbation, oral sex and homosexuality as morally valid, is shaping the nature and scope of sexuality education in Australia today. The dominant influence of such a sexual ideology can be both damaging and destructive to Muslim students and young people who do not identify with it. As Beckett (1996:15) points out, 'this way of thinking about standards of morality and goodness condemns other expressions of sex and sexuality as wrong and bad, which can have a profound effect on young people'. The contemporary approach that favours assimilation into the dominant culture rather than cultural pluralism so harbours a risk of indoctrination.

McKay (1997:288) asserts that in the face of ideological pluralism, indoctrination can be seen as a violation of basic human rights and, while it may not be possible to resolve what are fundamental conflicts of a plural society, 'a moral agenda for sex education may be the most appropriately realised' (ibid.:288). Australian school curricular and educational practices need to recognise and respect the reality, diversity and cultural specificity of student experiences in the classroom and address the sexual health educational needs of Muslim students. The sexual health education curriculum decision-making and development framework is therefore in urgent need of reform.

Developing a sexual health education curriculum framework for Muslim students

In my teaching experience at both mainstream and Victorian Islamic schools (Sanjakdar, 2000a), the curriculum development process essentially consists of sets of statements about what should or should not be included. Curriculum decision-making and development often begins with the review of external curriculum documents by senior school administrators, including the curriculum co-ordinator (See Figure 2). An accepted curriculum means the values and philosophies about goals, content and organisation in these documents are congruent with the school mission. These subjects then become the core curriculum, with time allocated to each in the timetable and resources purchased. A rejected curriculum becomes the null curriculum, 'the options students are not afforded, the perspectives they may never know about, much less be able to use, the concepts and skills that are not part of their intellectual repertoire' (Eisner, 1994:107). English texts, History topics and sexual health content that is viewed as controversial may be found in the null curriculum.

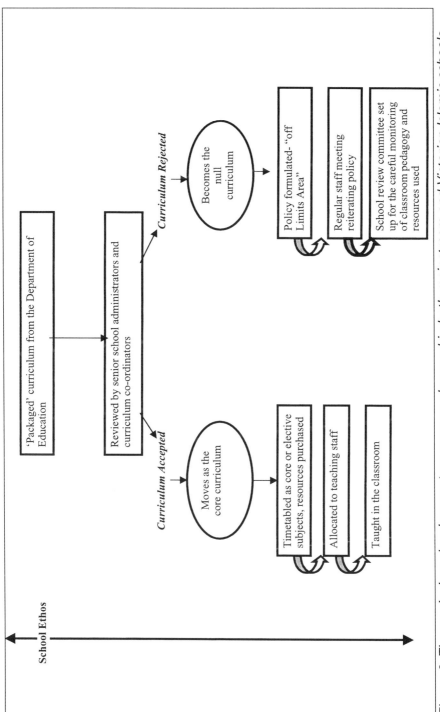

Figure 2: The curriculum development process as observed in both mainstream and Victorian Islamic schools

This linear pattern of curriculum development presents conceptual constraints for meeting the educational needs of Muslim
students in Australian schools. From an Islamic viewpoint, the
area of most concern is the total absence of a guiding religious
moral and values framework. Driven by pragmatic aims, knowledge is fragmented and compartmentalised, concerned only with
the intellectual and physical development of students. Underpinned by Western liberal values, the curriculum is devoid of any
others. Although the liberal values inherent in the sexual health
education curriculum reflect the actual political, legal and economic circumstances that prevail in Western societies generally
(Halstead and Reiss, 2003), there is a strong argument in the
literature for the inclusion of religious and cultural values in sexual
health education (Sears, 1997; Currie *et al.*, 1997). Ulanowsky
(1998) is outraged at how religion appears to be irrelevant in
health education today and sees this lack as implying hostility towards different worldviews. Halstead and Reiss (2003: 87) argue
that the lack of consideration in the sexual health curriculum for
the religious views of students in the classroom and broader
society fails to appreciate the universality and applicability of
religion to student lives.

> Religious views about sexual values need to be considered for two
> main reasons. First, that an inconsiderable number of people have
> them; second, that if we wish to live together in a pluralist society,
> it behoves all of us to understand at least something of what it is
> that motivates others. Such understanding is both intrinsically res-
> pectful and instrumentally useful.

Sexual health programmes that fail to recognise religious and cultural diversity are susceptible to a variety of 'breakdowns' (Irvine,
1995: xii) and misunderstandings, which are likely to occur across
lines of ethnic or other difference.

Such a curriculum framework has broad concerns about content
and outcomes. It falls short of describing, discriminating and establishing meanings that are related to what is valued in the curriculum, what is learned and what is achieved. Although all curriculum developers employ outcomes in some way when constructing curricula (Print, 1993), this developmental approach serves as

a lesson in the fallacy of the assumption that what *is*, is what *ought to be* (Brady and Kennedy, 1999: 100). An emphasis on outcomes based curriculum development also promotes a curriculum approach which tries to involve all students in sets of closed experiences and where the recipient, the student, remains essentially passive (Walker, 2003). This curriculum framework also creates a diversion from an examination of hegemony, thereby tacitly acting as an agent of social and cultural reproduction (Reid, 2002; Collins, 2002; Posner, 1995; Apple, 1993,1990; Giroux, 1981). The dominant role those who administer the curriculum exposes the absence of interaction between teachers, student and milieu, including parental groups and the wider community. As a result, dominant ideologies about knowledge become constructed, and teachers become an agent of these ideas, so discouraging the questioning of present conditions.

The remainder of this chapter presents a sexual health education curriculum framework for Muslim students. Based on my present study with Muslim teachers, it centres the role of culture in the construction of sexual health education and aims to:

• consider the implications of the current curriculum approach as well as the literature on Muslim parent and student concerns

• focus on both curriculum theory and practice

• offer a whole school approach to issues of ethnicity and sexuality

• be more inclusive of the needs of Muslim students but also flexible enough to incorporate multicultural perspectives on sexuality issues and sexuality education

• shed assumptions about what is considered 'normal' Australian behaviour and attitudes to sex and sexuality

• give schools the opportunity to plan for and include other controversial content in the curriculum, in a manner which reflects the school's own mission and ethos.

An appropriate curriculum framework

Developing a curriculum which effectively meets the needs of Muslim students for all subject areas including sexual health education must reflect the Islamic view of education. This is based on three important elements: the learner, knowledge and method of instruction. The relationship of these three is transformed here into three curriculum development processes: entirety, mediation and appropriation (see Figure 3).

Entirety

> Curriculum is not a concept, it is a cultural construction. It is not an abstract concept which has some existence outside and prior to human existence. (Grundy, 1987:5)

Although it is tempting to regard the curriculum as a private transaction between teacher and student, curriculum development is in fact both a personal and social construct, taking place in the much broader context of the social, political, economic and cultural structures of the school. When looking to serve the particular sexual health educational needs of Muslim students in a school context, curriculum planning must acknowledge the secular, pluralistic society in which Muslim students live and the culturally diverse nature of Australian Muslim society. Although Islam is a universal religion, Muslims do not constitute a homogenous group and whilst some Muslims views of education are strict, others can be quite liberal. Therefore curriculum development must take into

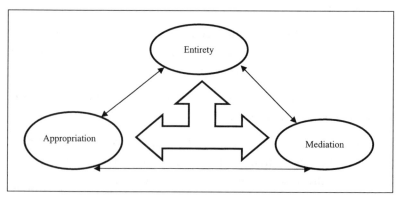

Figure 3: Towards developing an appropriate sexual health education curriculum for Muslim students

consideration the school ethos, culture, student population and background, parental and wider community – its 'entirety'.

Unlike the current curriculum decision-making and development process (see Figure 1), entirety shifts the focus from a curriculum embedded in statutory bodies or from an outside 'expert' source to one which vests interest and authority in the Muslim community or *ummah*, an approach consistent with the cultural patterns of Islam (Donohoue-Clyne, 2001). Although the curriculum is interwoven with the social fabric that sustains it, every school distinguishes between the common or core education, the universal elements of the wider society and the curriculum which meets the requirements within that culture. Based on this view, curriculum is concerned with maintaining its culture as a closely knit and well-integrated unit, constituting the moral content, regulating conduct and appropriate behaviour.

Applying the principle of entirety will:

- examine and consider the range of knowledge, assumptions, attitudes, values and expectations of the curriculum within the Muslim community
- help identify any constraints or barriers which may hinder the development and implementation of sexual health education
- encourage exploration of ways to engage students, parents and the wider community in designing educational practices which incorporate and respect Islamic viewpoints of modesty, Islamic behaviour, marriage and the family
- include the Muslim community in the political and social affairs of the school, attending to both educational and equity issues
- lead to a unity in curriculum production and a conceptually contextualised and holistic approach which is implicit in the Islamic viewpoint

Consideration of entirety would therefore provide a comprehensive and coordinated plan for intervention of health education at different levels of policymaking, programme administration and evaluation, manifesting into a knowledge platform where teachers and curriculum planners become prepared for mediation.

Mediation

Teachers are central to curriculum development and improvement (McNeil, 2003; Hatton, 1998; McGee, 1997). But many take an active role only in the enacted curriculum, which is often too late. From an Islamic point of view, the teacher is more important than the subject itself and learners should come in close contact with teachers and not rely mainly upon textbooks for knowledge. Mediation aims to give teaching and curriculum decision-making and development back to teachers. During this stage of curriculum development, teachers mediate on two levels; first with the current school structure and practices as embedded in its entirety and secondly, with each other.

Existing conditions tend to support existing practices. The first level of mediation will call attention to existing patterns of school organisation, classroom interaction and its embedded values. Mediation will:

- enrich and deepen the notion of the entirety by setting the conditions for curriculum development, including the establishment of a curriculum rationale that determines an appropriate values system and educational ideology
- allow for any possible constraints, as presented in the entirety, to be identified, removed or appropriately addressed
- provide teachers with the opportunity to interact with members of the Islamic community to refine their understanding of that particular group, to cultivate desire and motivation to work with them and to collect culturally relevant information to incorporate into curriculum development.

At the second level, teachers mediate their ideas and conceptions of the sexual health curriculum with one another. Teachers can be expected to teach from their own cultural experiences, so a teacher's conception of curriculum and classroom practice has implications for the knowledge made available to students (Hargreaves, 1995:10). Mediation allows teachers to discuss, listen to and examine one another's ideas in depth, making each sensitive to their own beliefs, values and bias. As teachers mediate, an equity culture is formed, where each teacher's contributions are heard and valued.

Mediation becomes the desirable vehicle for discussion on how the mechanisms of social and cultural reproduction both determine and legitimate the meaning of school arrangements, modes of knowing, ways of behaving and patterns of interaction. Mediation will also:

- enhance teacher participation, acceptance and motivation – a priority if effective curriculum development is to take place

- view the curriculum development process as a real life, on-going evolving process rather than a product

- help to break down school structures which tend to foster transmission, bureaucratisation and standardisation and position the school, teachers, the classroom and immediate environment as the best place for curriculum development.

Appropriation
Islam imposes no restrictions on the type and scope of knowledge for learning and teaching. All topics, subjects and discipline areas, including sexual health, are considered compulsory learning and an obligation incumbent upon every Muslim. Certain classroom pedagogy and practice in sexual health education has come under scrutiny by Muslim parents and students. Therefore, all curriculum content and teaching practice of sexual health for Muslim students must go through a process of appropriation. In this framework, appropriation is defined as making the modifications and changes to curriculum content and pedagogy so they become appropriate to Islamic teachings, beliefs and principles. This process involves consideration of the following:

- A shift in emphasis from the personal meanings and views of teachers to considering the way Islam views sexual health. This requires a grounding in Islamic scripture. While this is not possible in all Australian schools, a process of engaging and liaising with the community can promote critical dialogue and communication about Islam and sexual health. The teachers are not removed from this process and the interrelating of both entirety and mediation is emphasised.

- Considering the appropriation of existing classroom practices, texts, materials and resources. Respecting Islamic values in sexual health includes checking materials to ensure that they do not violate Islamic principles of modesty, decency, marriage and family life. From an Islamic viewpoint, pedagogy must be a contextualised process with a religious, moral and ethical motive and the Pedagogy of Prophet Muhammad (pbuh) can serve as an important guideline. The Prophet's (pbuh) practice as a teacher to his companions is the most important source of *shariah* (the religious and moral law of Islam). His tradition, including questioning to widen the area of conversation, using stories, narratives and parables, is considered the desirable pedagogy of Islamic education and the archetype of all necessary learning for Muslims (Al-Sadan, 1999).

- Sensitivity to the age and maturity of students. Sexual health education for Muslim students must be commensurate with age. Students are not supposed to know about the sexual act before they reach adolescence (Ashraf, 1998; Mabud, 1998) so great care is needed to ensure that school programmes do not undermine this.

Conclusion

The pluralistic nature of Australian society suggests that no one sexual ideology is poised to assume a hegemonic position. However, Australian schools and curricula transmit dominant cultures, values and ideologies and multicultural meanings are resisted and contested. Muslim students' necessary search for autonomy will lead them to question and challenge established norms and values. Although schools form only part of the influence on a young person's sexual health education and identity, they have a significant role.

While dominant adolescent culture tends to collude with permissive values, Muslim students must hold on to the thought that their religious values are relevant in modern society and not 'old fashioned' or 'bizarre'. Muslim students must be made to feel empowered by their religious beliefs and not controlled by a secular society. The aim of their sexual health education is to strengthen their faith and to counteract the sexual excesses of modern society, rather than being made to feel they have to 'adjust themselves to the situation and amend their religious code to suit the time' (Ashraf, 1998: 43).

A 'packaged' curriculum for sexual health education cannot anticipate local problems and possibilities. To actualise the aims of an Islamic education and provide relevant sexual health education to Muslim students, current Australian curriculum practices must change. The proposed sexual health education curriculum framework for Muslim students in schools situates the cultural contexts in which young people live, accommodates pluralism and allows for reformulating curriculum conceptions and reconstructing curriculum practice. The framework depends on maintaining congruence between the school and its entirety, encourages mediation between teachers and the appropriation of curriculum content and pedagogy. It indicates what a critical approach to inclusive curriculum might be and is a stance against the current forms of curriculum domination and its insensitivity to an Islamic context. Accommodating diverse religious and cultural values in sexual health is a step towards a productive and socially responsible curriculum, one that can give all students an opportunity to recognise others and develop a better understanding of themselves. A commitment to curricula which encourage learning about more than one culture can develop in educators the skills for working effectively with diversity.

11

Islamophobia before and after September 11th 2001

Lorraine Sheridan

Introduction

Prejudice and discrimination on religious grounds has received little attention from researchers, particularly when compared with the amount devoted to racial prejudice and discrimination. A brisk search of psychology's largest bibliographic database revealed that studies related to racial discrimination and prejudice currently outnumber similar works on religious discrimination and prejudice by eighteen to one. Other authors have also pointed out the dearth of academic and other materials on the subject of religious discrimination (e.g. Malik, 2001). And of the little work there is, virtually none has specifically examined the experiences of Muslims. This paucity of information makes it difficult to estimate and identify potential factors that may contribute to, exacerbate or alleviate Islamophobia.

The line that separates racial and religious discrimination is frequently indistinct (see Allen and Nielsen, 2002), which means that measures of the former can reveal the existence of the latter. For example, the 2000 British Crime Survey (Clancy *et al*, 2001) estimated that in 1999, Pakistanis and Bangladeshis suffered the highest crime victimisation rates of all England's and Wales' ethnic group. A high proportion of ethnic Pakistanis and Bangladeshis are Muslims, so one may speculate that some of this victimisation was provoked by religious differences.

This chapter reports the findings of a study that aimed to examine religious discrimination in a group of UK Muslims after the events of September 11th 2001. This was not the first to examine post September 11th Islamophobia. The European Monitoring Centre on Racism and Xenophobia (EUMC) anticipated a rise in Islamophobia after the attacks on the United States and so put in place a system to record anti Islamic reactions across all fifteen EU member states. Although variations in recording methods meant that reliable comparisons could not be made across all member states, Allen and Nielsen's (2002) summary report noted that Muslims had indeed experienced increased hostility post September 11th. Relatively low levels of physical violence were recorded; most common was verbal abuse, harassment and non verbal aggression. Some involved individuals whereas other attacks targeted groups or places such as mosques or Islamic cultural centres. Hate crimes such as abusive telephone calls, messages left on cars and anonymous letters to private homes were also reported. More generally, Islamophobic content was observed to increase in text messages and emails and on the Internet. The Muslim Council of Britain, for instance, received large numbers of abusive messages from individuals who sought to blame Muslims for the attacks on the US. At the same time, interest in Islamic culture increased – but did not always lead to greater understanding or acceptance of Islam and Muslims.

All this suggests that Islamophobia rose markedly after the events of September 11th. To what extent cannot be measured because there is no pre September 11th baseline. Allen and Nielsen (2002) suggest, however, that this increase did not represent a new phenomenon but that xenophobia and fear of Muslims recorded across many parts of the EU was rather an exacerbation of pre-existing sentiment, fuelled by feelings of fear and helplessness and a perceived threat of an 'enemy within'. They note that prejudicial attitudes tended to be localised within individual European states, which suggests that the events of September 11th were used to confirm or intensify historical prejudices.

Allen and Nielsen found that, throughout the EU, visible indications of possibly being Muslim was the primary factor in predicting who would be the victim of an Islamophobic attack or insult. This was found to be the case across all fifteen of the EU member states. The predominant visual identifier appeared to be the hijab or headscarf and more women were targeted. Other groups were also made vulnerable by virulent Islamophobia. Sikh men wearing turbans were also targeted, presumably because of a perceived resemblance to Osama bin Laden, suspected of orchestrating the attacks on the World Trade Center and the Pentagon. In the United States, a man was sentenced to death for murdering a Sikh he took to be an Arab four days after these attacks, apparently in revenge. As mosques and other buildings used by Muslims were the targets of vandalism, graffiti, arson and bomb attacks, Allen and Nielsen conclude that what appeared to be important was whether attackers perceived their target to be Islamic, whether or not it was.

Figures complied by the Federal Bureau Investigation (FBI) suggest that hate crimes against Arabs and Muslims in the US increased by 1,700 per cent in 2001. In 2000, the FBI received reports of 28 hate crimes against Muslims and Arabs as against 481 in 2001. In Australia, Dunn (2003) asked 5056 respondents whether they believed any ethnic or cultural groups did not fit into Australian society. Forty-five per cent identified one or more such groups, with Muslims and people from the Middle East most frequently named. At least 635 respondents named Muslims and 641 indicated people from the Middle East. When asked how they would feel should a close relative marry someone Aboriginal Australian, Asian, British, Christian, Italian, Jewish or Muslim, the most overwhelmingly negative responses related to Muslims. For instance, 14.7 per cent of respondents said they would be extremely concerned should a close relative marry a Muslim, but only 3.2 per cent had similar feelings about Asians. Anti-Muslim sentiment, then, is prevalent across parts of Europe, the US and Australia. Still not determined is the extent of Islamophobia in other countries, for example India and African nations that share their borders with majority Muslim nations.

Several studies have examined religious discrimination in specifically educational contexts. In a study of Hindu, Indian Muslim and Pakistani children who attended school in Lancashire, Eslea and Mukhtar (2000) found that 57 per cent of boys and 43 per cent of girls aged twelve to fifteen (of a sample of 243) had been bullied during a single school term. In all cases the bullying was likely to have been related to religious or cultural differences. Inter-Asian as well as White-Asian bullying was seen, as Hindu children most frequently bullied Pakistani and Indian Muslim children. In higher education establishments in the US, Omeish (1999) found that Muslim students perceived religious prejudice and discrimination to be a common feature of their educational experience.

A study commissioned by the Home Office (Weller *et al*, 2001) investigated religious discrimination across more than twenty different faith groupings in England, using questionnaire data and meetings and interviews with representatives from each faith group. The researchers concluded that indifferent attitudes towards and ignorance of religion were widespread across England and Wales. The Muslim organisations that took part in the study reported generally higher levels of ill treatment than did the other faith group organisations, both relatively and absolutely. In addition, Muslims were most likely to state that their experience of religious discrimination had intensified since 1996.

A majority of Muslim organisations in the Weller *et al* investigation reported that the people they represented experienced unfair treatment in education, employment, housing, law and order and in relation to local government services. For almost every aspect of education that the survey addressed, the authors found that Muslim, Sikh and Hindu organisations reported higher levels of unfair treatment than Christian, Jewish, Buddhist and Baha'i organisations. While a majority of Christian and Jewish organisations reported occasional unfair treatment, Muslims were more likely to report frequent ill treatment. They reported being treated unfairly in certain aspects of education: admissions, curriculum, dress, holidays, marginalisation and timetabling. Unfair treatment at the hands of both students and staff was described, as well as unfair treatment from education officials due to the policies and practices of education authorities.

These findings are particularly disturbing since, as research has shown, education experiences can influence discriminatory attitudes in at least three ways. First, educational establishments can directly affect ethnic, racial, cultural and religious association. Second, young people are exposed to the attitudes of teachers and lecturers, whether positive or negative. Finally, the educational curriculum may covertly or overtly perpetuate or challenge stereotypes. The hidden curriculum may subtly promote or reflect prejudicial attitudes. For instance, school textbooks in the US have been shown to demean minorities and play down the negative impact of historical events on minority groupings (e.g. Oakes, 1985). Turbes *et al* (2002) demonstrated that medical training can needlessly highlight racial or culturally 'specific' diseases and Margolis and Romero (1998) found that their postgraduate sociology students easily identified racial stereotypes portrayed in their curriculum. More positively, other work has identified that teachers may be able to use the hidden curriculum to promote positive attitudes towards, for instance, hard work and sexual and racial equality (Kanpol, 1989).

The remainder of this chapter details the results of a study that examined negative experiences based on religious and racial differences in a sample of British Muslims. Respondents were asked about their experiences both before 9/11 and after. Because many individuals disguise racist attitudes to appear to conform to social niceties (see e.g. Dovidio and Fazio, 1991) the study focused on both general discriminatory experiences and more subtle kinds in which people exhibit racist or Islamophobic sentiments while denying any prejudice.

The study
Respondents and their home cities
Between October and December 2001, a questionnaire was distributed among Muslims in two English towns, Leicester and Stoke-on-Trent. It was posted on the Internet. Contacts with mosques, cultural centres and religious organisations identified possible respondents.

There were 222 respondents, all describing themselves as Muslim. Over half (53%) were female, average age 22 years. The largest proportion was aged under 40. Almost a third (36%) were aged 13 to 19, and another 53 per cent were aged 20 to 29. Just under 10 per cent were between 30 and 39, and 2.5 per cent between 40 and 46. The highest proportion of participants (62%) described themselves as Pakistani. The next largest ethnic group described themselves as Indian (13%), followed by those who were ethnically Bangladeshi (8%), White (8%), Other Asian (5%), and Arab (4%). One participant was Indian/White and one was Black.

More than half the respondents (60%) were born in the United Kingdom. The next most frequent country of birth was Pakistan (19%), followed by Bangladesh (3%). Between one and four participants were born in each of the following countries: Azerbaijan, Denmark, Egypt, Greece, India, Kuwait, Malaysia, Palestine, Saudi Arabia, Somalia, Sri Lanka and Zimbabwe. An additional 10% declined to state their country of birth. The vast majority of the 222 respondents (80%) were UK citizens. The next most frequent country of citizenship was Pakistan (5%), followed by Saudi Arabia (1%). Eight per cent declined to state their country of citizenship.

According to the 2001 population census, 60.54 per cent of the population of Leicester was White, and 25.73 per cent of Indian origin. People of Pakistani origin represented 1.53 per cent. Leicester is an ethnically diverse British town and has the largest Indian population of any local authority area in England and Wales. The Muslim population of Leicester was estimated by the 2001 census to be 11.03 per cent, compared to a national average of 2.97 per cent. The Muslim presence in Leicester had risen from the 4.3 per cent estimated in 1983. Stoke-on-Trent, on the other hand, was reported by the 2001 census to have a white population of 94.8 per cent, and a Muslim population of 3.2 per cent, close to national averages. In Leicester, Hinduism is the largest non-Christian religion and Indian the largest most non-white ethnicity, whilst in Stoke Islam is the largest non-Christian religion and Pakistani the largest ethnic minority. Thus, the study described here drew its sample from two towns with contrasting populations.

The socio economic status of participants, as defined by their occupational title, was as follows: over half were University, college or sixth form students (53 per cent), 14 per cent attended secondary school, 6 per cent were housewives, 4 per cent were professionals, 4 per cent worked in customer services and a further 4 per cent were unemployed. The remainder were employed in unskilled or semi skilled work, were administrators, worked in retail, were technicians, health workers, or were self-employed (14 per cent in all).

The questionnaire

The questionnaire was constructed specifically for the study and consisted of an introduction and four main sections. Extra sheets were provided to allow participants to make further comments. The introduction informed respondents that the purpose of the study was to increase knowledge about the range of racism-related experiences that people have, particularly since September 11th 2001. Anonymity and confidentiality was assured, and the individual's identity could not be linked in any way to their completed questionnaire. The rest of the questionnaire is detailed below.

Section one – general information: participants indicated on a scale their frequency of attendance at religious services, their visibility as a Muslim, their ethnic origin, and the proportion of their neighbourhood sharing their religious beliefs and ethnic origin.

Section two – racism and religious discrimination of a covert nature: nineteen questionnaire items measured experiences of covert racism and religious discrimination. Respondents were asked how often they had had such experiences purely because of their race, ethnicity or religion (i) during a typical year and (ii) since the attacks on the US. All nineteen experiences delineated were based on daily life situations and designed to reflect the incidence of covert rather than overt racism and religious discrimination. So they included: being treated in an overly friendly or superficial manner, being treated with suspicion or being wrongly accused, being avoided or having others physically move away, and being asked to speak for one's entire ethnic, racial or religious group. The aim was to focus participants' memory on *differences* in the incidence of these items before and after September 9/11. Thus, respondents were first asked to indicate how often they had had these experiences during a typical year and then to indicate whether these nineteen experiences had occurred less often than, the same as, or more often, than usual.

Section three – general discrimination: participants were asked about their experiences of general discrimination via fourteen items which typified the more overt and transparent forms of racial and religious discrimination, such as seeing negative stereotypes of one's ethnic or religious group in the media, experiencing a racially hostile atmosphere at work or in the educational setting, violent or life threatening experiences, and significant racial or religiously fuelled tensions in the local community. These items measured direct experience or observation of discriminatory practices on the grounds of the respondents' race, ethnicity or religion. As in section two, respondents were asked how often they had such experiences before September 11 and after so the frequency of these experiences could be gaged. Questionnaire items were partially drawn from the project, *Through my Eyes: Perceptions and Experiences of Racism*, conducted by Shelley P. Harrell and Hector Myers of the University of California.

Section four – specific incidents: participants were asked to describe in some detail any incident of religious discrimination or racism that they knew or suspected to be related to the events of September 11. Descriptions were included for analysis if they met two criteria: that they were unambiguously related to the events of September 11, and that the participant was involved as a victim.

Findings
Post September 11 changes in covert racism and religious discrimination
A minority of respondents (11 per cent) recorded an overall decrease in their experience of covert racism and religious discrimination after 9/11, and a further 6 per cent did not report any change. Most repondents however (83 per cent) did report increases. Table 1 lists all fourteen questionnaire items that set out to measure covert dircrimination, and indicates the proportion of the sample who reported an increasing in experiences of them.

Table 1: The rise in experience of covert racism and religious discrimination

Nature of experiences	Percentage of sample reporting increases
Hearing/being told an offensive joke	73.8
Being stared at by strangers	68.2
Being asked to speak for entire racial/religious group	53.9
Being insulted/harassed/verbally abused	51.6
Being treated rudely	46.6
Being closely observed or followed in public	46.6
Others reacting as if intimidated or afraid	46.6
Being treated as stupid	43.4
Being ignored/overlooked/refused service	42.3
Being avoided, or seeing others move away	42.2
Being treated in an overly friendly/superficial manner	40.2
Having ideas/opinions devalued or ignored	39.4
Being treated with suspicion or being wrongly accused	37.1
Being laughed at or taunted	33.1
Not being taken seriously	32.7
Being expected to produce inferior work	30.8
Being excluded from conversation or activities	29.1
Being considered fascinating/exotic	25.2
Being mistaken for member of another racial/religious group	18.7

Table 1 shows that all fourteen of the forms of racism became more prevalent after 9/11. Almost three quarters of respondents reported hearing more offensive jokes. Over two thirds of participants reported being stared at by strangers more frequently. The next greatest increases involved being asked to speak for one's entire racial or religious group, and being insulted or called a rude name.

Changes in general racism and religious discrimination after 9/11

Some respondents (15 per cent) reported a decrease in their experiences of general discrimination and 9 per cent indicated no significant change. As with experiences of more covert discrimination however, the majority of participants (76 per cent) reported an overall increase. Table 2 lists all fourteen questionnaire items and demonstrates that all increased significantly after 9/11.

It is clear from Table 2 that hearing offensive or insensitive remarks increased most of all after September 11, while Table 1 records that the greatest escalation among the more covert items was hearing offensive jokes. Islamophobia in the form of insensitive jokes and offensive remarks rose significantly. Table 2 also indicates the observed increases in negative or insulting stereotypes of Muslims in the media. Being subjected to offensive

Table 2: The rise in experiences of a kind generally discriminatory

Nature of experience	Percentage of sample reporting post 9/11 increases
Hearing offensive or insensitive remarks	66.7
Observing negative or insulting stereotypes in the media	63.8
Hearing about discrimination or prejudice towards others	61.6
Observing exclusory or negative political practices	56.4
Racial/religious tensions or conflicts in community	55.3
Observing exclusory or negative practices at work or school	48.9
Being expected to conform to racial or religious stereotype	47.9
Witnessing discrimination or prejudice towards others	47.5
Observing exclusory problems regarding health, employment etc.	47.0
Hateful or mean-spirited behaviour	36.1
Conflict with person of different religion/race/ethnicity	33.8
Hostile atmosphere due to racial/religious differences	28.4
Others inferring paranoia over religious discrimination/racism	24.7
Violent or life-threatening experiences	17.8

remarks is hurtful but there is often little recourse for the victim. Table 2 also shows that almost 18 per cent of respondents reported an increase in violent or life-threatening experiences and many said they did not inform the police because they felt that little could be done to apprehend the perpetrators.

If these figures reflect the wider population they are alarming. The 2000 British Crime Survey revealed that of all racial groups, Bangladeshis and Pakistanis were most likely to be victims of violent crime. More research is needed to ascertain the proportion of violence motivated by religious discrimination. Until religious discrimination becomes a mainstream topic of research, it will always be subservient to issues of race. Although participants in the current study indicated such a big increase in violent and life-threatening experience, almost a quarter said they were more likely to be told that they were being paranoid when they complained about discrimination and prejudice.

Specific incidents

The respondents were asked to describe a single incident of discriminatory or hateful behaviour in detail and specifically about acts they suspected or knew to be related to the September 11 attacks. Only the decriptions of experiences judged to be unequivocally related to the attacks were included in the analysis, and only those in which the respondents themselves were the primary victims. In all, almost a fifth of the sample (19.8 per cent) reported an incident of this kind.

Statistical analyses confirmed no significant correlation existed between whether or not an incident was reported and the following variables: country of birth or citizenship, ethnicity, frequency of religious attendance, marital status, occupation, and the individual's visibility as a Muslim. This was somewhat surprising, especially since previous work had identified visibility as a Muslim to be the most important predictive factor of whether someone was the victim of a an Islamophobic attack after 9/11 (Allen and Nielsen, 2002). Allen and Nielsen's work identified that women were more likely to suffer abuse than men, probably because wearing the hijab makes them immediately recognisable as Muslims. The male and female respondents discussed here however, were almost equally likely to report a specific abusive incident (18.6 per cent of females; 21.2 per cent of males) and their accounts showed clearly that the perpetrators were deliberately targeting Muslims.

Also surprising was that ethnicity was found to be unrelated to whether or not an Islamophobic incident was reported. Ethnic Arab, Bangladeshi, Black, Indian, Pakistani, White, Other Asian, and mixed race Muslims were equally likely to record specific discriminatory experiences. Those identified as possible perpetrators of the 9/11 attacks on the US are primarily Arab. This finding provides further evidence that respondents were reporting instances of Islamophobia rather than racial discrimination.

Given the youth of the sample (average age 22 years), many were in full-time education. Like the street, public transport, commercial centres and the workplace, educational establishments were not immune to post 9/11 Islamophobic incidents. Several respondents informed the study, in their own words, of incidents that occurred in schools, colleges and Universities. One school student wrote:

> ...in school, where nobody ever inquired on my racial background, students began to express curiosity on my race/religion. I was asked many times after 11 September if I was born in Afghanistan or had any links with the Taliban or Osama bin Laden! I strongly believe that Muslims are being put under tension for irrelevant reasons. *Female school student, age 15*

Another spoke more generally about Islamophobic feeling at her school:

> Since the attacks on the World Trade Center have taken place I have noticed that Muslims have been treated badly. I have witnessed events at school such as fights where the white students have always started and caused problems first. *Female school student, age 14*

One student observed that the attacks on 9/11 had aggravated already existing difficulties in her college:

> ...I think the severity of the trouble has increased since the attacks on America as they hold one single group responsible. This can cause tensions and arguments, especially when there are many different points of view in one community. *Female student, age 18*

Respondents also reported incidents involving teachers:

> At school, a teacher turned around to another teacher of a dark colour who was not of my religion. She came out with the remark 'I hate Muslims – they are a waste of time and space and they cause trouble all the time'. The school has a small population of Asian/ Muslim/Sikh/Hindu children. This particular teacher has five in her class. *Female nursery nurse, age 23*

Cases where staff failed to intervene were also noted, for instance:

> When I was at college I heard a girl saying that Muslims should be killed. Then that way they will definitely get the killers. The lecturer overheard but did nothing. *Male student, age 17*

Other respondents reported about the post-educational implications of Islamophobia:

> I am currently looking for a job, and before the attacks on the World Trade Centre, I have already felt that I am being discriminated [against] due to my ethnic background, and that I am treated differently because of this. Since the attacks on the World Trade Centre, I am afraid to mention on my CV that I was an active member of my University's Islamic Society, or to tell that I am a Muslim, for fear of being looked at as though I am a terrorist. I feel that this would increase if was to wear a hijab. I went for an interview recently, and was asked what other things I did at University, and I mentioned that I was a member of the Islamic Society, and felt that the tone of the lady interviewing me had changed. Many people see Muslims as the evil in the world since September 11 and they only generalise from extreme groups which are distortions of Islam. *Female PhD student, age 24*

Conclusions

The study described in this chapter found that a sample of 222 Muslims reported large rises after 9/11 in abuse and discrimination and in covert, subtle indications of prejudice. Although the frequency increased significantly, many respondents had experienced Islamophobic sentiment prior to the events of September 11 2001. As Allen and Nielson (2002) observe, the attacks on the US did not set in motion a major problem but rather exacerbated an existing one. The nature of the prejudice respondents described varied widely, from newspaper reports to verbal abuse to serious physical assault. Neither were the contexts uniform. Islamophobic behaviour occurred in public, at work, in their neighbourhood, on public transport, at home and in educational establishments.

Islamophobia in education is perhaps particularly repellent. Education can enlighten students and promote positive attitudes. Many studies in the social sciences have demonstrated that educated people are usually more tolerant. Education settings can be the first arena in which battles can be fought against Islamophobia. It is to education that our attention should be directed.

12

Self in Society and Society in Self: encounters between Jewish and Arab students in Israel

Shifra Sagy, Shoshana Steinberg and Mouin Fahiraladin

Introduction

Thе purpose of this chapter is to evaluate two types of intergroup encounters as a means to decrease animosity and increase the potential for coexistence between two groups, in this case two distinct cultures – a Jewish majority and an Arab minority – living in one country, Israel. The findings have consequences for educators seeking to resolve conflicts between groups that are experiencing tension. Here we examine intergroup encounters in which Israeli Jewish and Arab students attending an Israeli university met to work on the Israeli-Arab political conflict. A qualitative analysis was undertaken, based on ethnographic data collected from two workshops over the course of two academic years. A major dilemma in intergroup encounters is the tension between a salient group identity on the one hand and personal and interpersonal characteristics on the other. In the analysis we explore what kind of balance between the two can lead to changes in attitudes and intergroup relations. Should emphasis be placed on the individual or the group? The research questions are analysed in the context of topics central to the Jewish-Arab conflict, such as the Holocaust and Al-Nakba (the Palestinian term for the 1948 war, meaning the Big Disaster).

Jewish and Arab encounter groups in Israel

Encounters between Jewish and Arab university students have been taking place in Israel since the early 1980s. They have focused on the tense relationship and the possibility of coexistence between the two primary cultures of Israel (Amir and Ben-Ari, 1989; Bargal and Bar, 1996; Katz and Kahanof, 1990). Reviews of such encounters discuss the tension between the political-group dimension and the psychological-personal and interpersonal dimension, usually to link to the declared and hidden goals of group participants and initiators.

The goals of these encounters were usually dichotomous (Katz and Kahanof, 1990; Suleiman, 1996). On the micro level, the initiators wanted to develop interpersonal closeness and relationships between the participants as individuals, so avoided references to political issues that might fuel controversy. But since the goal at a macro level was to find solutions to a socio-national conflict, political issues and the outside reality had to be stressed. How to reconcile the tension between these two 'oppositional' demands?

Most researchers (e.g., Rouhana and Korper, 1997; Sonnenschein et al, 1998; Suleiman, 1996) have explained the tension in terms of a power struggle between a minority group and a majority group.

An alternative approach explores the cultural differences between Jews and Arabs (Sagy, 2000). Culture can affect the precise content and structure of the inner self (Markus and Kitayama, 1991) as well as the definition of self and the complexity of the private versus collective selves (Marsella et al, 1985; Triandis, 1989). A few studies have found Arab-Israelis to be more likely than Jewish-Israelis to generate selves focused on national-religious ethnic collective groups (Oyserman, 1993; Sagy et al, 2001). The likelihood that Arab-Israeli participants will focus on the collective self in intergroup encounters may reflect the more collectivistic-orientation of Arab culture.

The interactionist approach sees the situational context as important in understanding the tension between the personal and political self. We did not find studies of Jewish and Arab encounters that adopted an interactionist explanation. And we found no answer to the question, 'What in the encounter situation itself strengthens group identity vis-à-vis the individual self?'

This chapter examines two types of intergroup encounters between Jewish and Arab Israeli students and asks:

• which selves were more salient in the situations studied?

• What in each encounter contributed to the salience of group identity versus the personal self?

• How does the difference in salience contribute to achievement of the encounters' goals?

Method

The analysis focuses on two kinds of encounters, or workshops, conducted with students from Ben Gurion University of the Negev. The University workshop was a series of meetings, spaced throughout one academic year (1996/7 and 1997/8), initiated by lecturers in the Education Department and led by two facilitators (an Arab and a Jew) from the School for Peace (Neve Shalom). Sixteen students (8 Arabs and 8 Jews) participated in 1996/7 and 19 (10 Arabs and 9 Jews) in 1997/8. The participants were completing their undergraduate or graduate studies in various departments. The group met once a week for three hours and once every three weeks within their own cultural group. The group meetings were observed by two lecturers (including Shifra Sagy) and a doctoral student (Shoshana Steinberg) from behind a one way mirror. Steinberg recorded the audio and video proceedings, and had them fully transcribed. Participants in the University workshops kept personal diaries in which they described their impressions, thoughts and feelings during each meeting and these were collected at the end of the year.

The Frankfurt workshop was a one-off event which took place as part of a student exchange project with Goethe University in Frankfurt. Although all the participants in the Frankfurt workshop had taken part in one of the two university workshops, this encounter was self-contained. It involved thirteen students (7 Arabs and 6 Jews), not all of whom were acquainted before going to Germany. Two lecturers from Goethe University and Sagy from Ben Gurion University initiated the Frankfurt workshop and the facilitators from Neve Shalom, who had led the University workshops, conducted it. The meetings were recorded and transcribed by Steinberg. Since the technical conditions of the meetings were unsuitable for observation, the authors participated in the group meetings. The visit lasted from 9-16 October, 1998. There were tours and lectures highlighting the multicultural aspects of Frankfurt and a visit to the Buchenwald concentration camp and also spontaneous informal evenings of dancing, singing, trips in the woods, outings and so on. Participants in the Frankfurt Workshop filled out open-ended questionnaires during the flights to and from Germany. The first questionnaire referred to the project's goals – as the students perceived them – their reasons for participating, expectations and evaluation of the itinerary of the visit. On the flight home, the participants were asked about the attainment of the project's aims, their fulfillment of personal expectations and what had been especially meaningful or irrelevant, annoying or boring.

The workshops were analysed using an inductive approach to identify how the participants constructed their personal individual identity as opposed to – or together with – their collective group identity. We did not use predetermined categories for analysis but looked for meaningful themes that came up during the encounters. Sagy collected additional data at a summary meeting, three weeks after the group returned.

There follows an analysis of some of the findings, including quotes from the participants' oral and written statements, and a comparison of the two different situations in which the encounters took place.

Analysis of the encounters

The analysis here focuses on:

- the salience of the collective self versus the personal self: attitudes of the initiators, the facilitators, and the participants. How do the participants think the discussions should be conducted?

- how the central and emotionally-charged issues of the Holocaust and Al-Nakba were dealt with in the groups

The salience of the collective self versus the personal self

The goals of the University and Frankfurt workshops were similar, integrating aims on personal, interpersonal and intergroup levels. The workshops were not intended to resolve concrete conflicts in the external world but to help people understand them and propose strategies and approaches to cope with them (Bar and Eady, 1998). This included developing the participants' awareness of the complexity of the Jewish-Arab conflict and their personal role in it, and enabling them to explore and construct their identity through interaction with the 'other side'. The encounters sought to develop ways of communicating that would facilitate intergroup and interpersonal dialogue, in the belief that awareness and consciousness enable people to choose their way according to their understanding, and that a clear, mature identity fosters relationships based on mutuality and equality (Helms, 1990; Phinney, 1990).

Although the workshop initiators and the Neve Shalom facilitators agreed on common goals, they did not agree on a strategy for achieving them. Neve Shalom emphasises strategies at group and collective level (Halabi and Sonnenschein, 1999) and the facilitators based their workshops on the assumption that group differentiation and preservation of group boundaries were necessary for solutions from the workshops to be made applicable to the external environment (Hewstone and Brown, 1986).

In contrast, the lecturers' approach was more integrative, emphasising both the collective and the personal elements of self. They advocated their approach in the weekly discussions with the facilitators about how to 'uncover' the personal stories of the participants and required the students to write personal diaries, interview family members and so on. This integrative approach was used more in the Frankfurt Workshop.

In the University workshop, however, the facilitators' approach prevailed, starting when the Arab facilitator introduced himself thus:

> We shall refer here to the relations between the two groups: Jews and Arabs. We presume that what is happening here represents what is happening outside. We are two facilitators: a Jew and an Arab. We look upon the reality in terms of a majority/minority relationship.

The facilitation continued by focusing only on the interaction and intergroup processes. The facilitators interpreted, reflected and explained the processes that occurred between the two groups. and linked these to the outside reality, paying no attention to the interpersonal interactions between individuals. They perceived interpersonal interactions as inhibiting the understanding of intergroup relations. Participants were usually treated as spokespeople for their own group, even when they expressed a personal opinion. Did facilitation of this kind lead to the salience of the group and the group identity? What were the results of the university encounters?

Analyses of the workshops show that group identity was indeed the dominant style. The participants saw themselves as representatives of their group and their counterparts as representatives of the other group. The discussions took place mostly on the macro ideological – political level. Discussions emphasised a feeling of one group against another, and consisted of arguments and counter arguments. Mutual accusations and group defensiveness were prevalent. Aspects of the conflict dominated discussion. Moreover, the salient discourse in the group reflected the extreme national and uncompromising voice. Those who wanted to stand out in the group adopted the position that would attract attention. A rare example of invoking personal stories was Fatma's (Arab female) story:

> Machmoud (an Arab male participant) said that our solution will be a political solution. I have a personal story, it's not political.

(My) roommate ... is Jewish and in the beginning of our relationship she talked about equality. She said she voted for Meretz (a left-wing party), and her behaviour is modern. Last week she was in our room. She came in with her mother. Her mother, incidentally, is a special education teacher. They didn't know I was upstairs. My roommate just sat there with her mother and they started to talk about how stupid the Arab girls are. My roommate talked about me and said that I am a special education teacher in the Bedouin schools. In the Bedouin schools there are not enough qualified teachers for special education. I am a sociology student, so I am (not) qualified to be a teacher in special education. My roommate's mother said: 'If I was the principal and she was a special education teacher, I would dismiss her the first day.' She started to say that Arab girls are stupid ... I was so angry that I cried. It's not that she's talking about me. I am self-aware. I know that I am an intelligent person and that I am educated and self-confident. But I was angry about the fact that she said she voted for Meretz and that she believed in equality when in her inner self she perceived us like this.

This was the sole attempt to tell a personal story. Responses to it apparently gave Fatma, and others, the feeling that personal stories were irrelevant for intergroup encounters.

During a Jewish-only workshop, Hannit was asked to tell her personal story – a dramatic personal testimony about a suicide bombing – at the next mutual workshop. But she refused, probably because the context, in which there was strong group salience, inhibited her from doing so, even though her story related to topics discussed in the workshop.

In the Frankfurt workshop, the facilitators still stressed intergroup salience during the discussions, but other messages emerged also. The students lived together during the entire encounter, and this inevitably affected the relationships among the participants. Also, since their was no one-way mirror where the university staff could observe the workshop, they sat in the room and sometimes found themselves involved in the discussions – mainly by sending messages which emphasised the salience of individual identity, encouraging the students to tell personal stories when appropriate. This new situation generated a different kind of discussion. For example, in the first meeting in Frankfurt, Hannit told her personal story:

> I often felt like a stranger at the (University) workshop. I experienced pain because my parents were injured by Arabs. It was important for me that the Arabs will understand ... We need a country of our own because of the need for security... In the workshop I always felt that 'You, the Jews are wrong', and where am I? Not many people have experienced what I endured.

One reason Hannit decided to go to Germany was to take the opportunity to express her individual personal identity in the intergroup encounter. She said she had been unaware of this feeling before the trip but felt it in the first group meeting in Frankfurt.

The need to touch on the individual self was sometimes expressed in the students' personal diaries:

> 'I personally was angry at these guys in the workshop who thought that the personal discussion was unnecessary. We are not machines. Our daily lives consist of these small experiences, which are the most important and influential for us, and not the political decisions of the government.' (Arab female)

> '...I am sometimes tired of talking in the workshop about these big things, and I feel more and more that I prefer to talk during the breaks, 'one on one'.' (Jewish female)

To sum up, the analysis of the discussions and the diaries seem to reveal a preference for discussion at Frankfurt on the individual rather than group level, probably because of the situational contexts. It distinguished the men from the women, more than it distinguished the Jews from the Arabs – an observation which contradicts other reviews, for example, Suleiman (1996). Each individual belongs to various social categories simultaneously – gender, economic status, area of residence, etc – and not only one – cultural – category (Doise et al, 1978).

The Holocaust and Al-Nakba: two central and emotionally charged issues

The memory of the Holocaust is central to the construction of Jewish Israeli identity, existing in the Jewish consciousness and in the collective memory as an historical traumatic event on both the individual and group level. The collective memory of the helplessness of the Jewish victims has created a Jewish Israeli ethos of needing security and military strength.

Among the Palestinians, Al-Nakba and its outcomes have played a dominant and formative role in how Palestinians construct their collective memory. Kimmerling (1999) goes so far as to liken it to the memory of the Holocaust for Jews. Arab popular culture has been created around issues related to Al-Nakba and is connected to the past, present and future. These images include the memory of the lost Garden of Eden from which the Arabs were evicted, the mourning of the present situation, and the will to take revenge, while visualising the future return to Palestine. The Palestinians see themselves as victims of the Holocaust, not only indirectly, due to the UN's decision to compensate the Jewish victims of the Nazis by giving them a part of Palestine, but because the Israelis use 'Nazi tactics' and 'racist aggression' (Kimmerling, 1999).

While it is essential for people to understand the significance of the Holocaust to Jewish-Israelis, knowing about Al-Nakba is essential for understanding Arab suffering. We believe that mutual recognition is essential for real dialogue.

The emotionally-charged issues of the Holocaust and Al-Nakba came up in both workshops but the discussions were entirely different.

When one of the University workshops coincided with the 40th anniversary of a massacre by Israeli soldiers of Arab civilians who violated curfew in Kfar Kassem, Samir (Arab male) raised the topic of the Holocaust by addressing the Jews as a group:

> Samir: 'Today is the 40th anniversary of the Kfar Kassem Massacre. I wonder how much you are interested in this subject.'

He makes no distinction between individuals, using the collective form 'you'. Samir's words suggest that the Jewish group might be indifferent, uninformed and uninterested in Arab history. Immediately after this, however, he shifted to more interpersonal dialogue: 'I would like to know, for instance, that if you were to see me walking on the campus while there was a siren for Holocaust

Memorial Day, how would you look at me?' Samir was trying to compare the Holocaust to the Kfar Kassem Massacre, both in the past and the present, by means of interpersonal discourse.

Avner (Jewish male): 'It would disturb me very much'.

Although the response is personal ('me'), its content is ethnocentric. Although Avner believes that the Arab Israelis should respect the memory of the Holocaust, the Kfar Kassem massacre clearly does not interest him. Avner's response reveals his opposition to any comparison between the Holocaust and the wrongs done to Arab Israelis. There is no expression of interest, empathy, sorrow, or any emotional response that indicates that he had listened to the message conveyed by the 'other', the Arab participant.

Later, the conversation moved back to the intergroup level, expressing growing disconnection between the two groups and a reluctance or incapacity to understand the other's perspective:

Samir: 'I want to know how much...'

Avner: 'How much I am aware?'

Samir: 'No, your awareness does not interest me, because you should worry about it and not I. The question is if you relate to issues the same way ... to what extent do you treat the two issues, the Holocaust and the Kafar Kassem Massacre in the same way?'

As the discussion continued, the accusations, disconnection, and unwillingness to understand the other's perspective increased, and the mood worsened.

Another workshop involving these issues took place on Holocaust Memorial Day. This encounter was characterised primarily by long silences, showing the difficulty the participants had dealing with the subject and the feeling that discussion between the two groups on the subject was impossible. For example:

Samir (Arab male): '...You are trying ... you know how to use the Holocaust very well, beyond the feeling of sorrow, beyond the feeling of pain that you feel. It is beyond, absolutely much beyond.'

Lihi (Jewish female): 'But you cannot understand somehow how we feel.'

Layla (Arab female): 'According to many facts, what happened in the Holocaust, according to much evidence, many things that happened there are not as told.'

Lihi (Jewish female): 'I don't think that this is the point for discussion at all.'

Rachel, Layla's Jewish friend, wrote in her diary after this meeting:

I felt, during the encounter, that I am drifting further and further away from them, and there is no way back. The things influenced me so strongly and deeply that later on it was hard for me to meet them in the university hallways. The meeting on Holocaust Memorial Day placed a barrier between us which is impossible to remove. The things that Layla said hurt me most. This meeting, especially, distanced me from her, because there was something to get away from ... This meeting made me feel that something had changed ... the distance between us is too big for us even to be citizens of the same country ... From this encounter I reached the cynical conclusion that everyone is for himself.

Saida (Arab female) wrote:

The silence of the Jews was very strong. Its force was stronger than the talking ... It is hard for the Jews to talk about the Holocaust with the Arabs. The distance was very great. This was one of the meetings where I felt that we are not talking, that the other side is immersed in its own pain and that there is no use in talking or that the meeting is irrelevant, since we will not be able to understand!

In another University workshop, Nasser (Arab male) compared Jewish Israeli soldiers' behaviour in the occupied territories to the Nazis' deeds in the Holocaust:

Avner (Jewish male): 'Nasser compared the incident with the soldiers to the Holocaust, and it annoys me.'

Nasser (Arab male): 'It annoys you when the Holocaust is mentioned because you are the one who is responsible?'

Avner: 'The Holocaust is a totally different historical event ... It was a systematic destruction of people...'

Nasser: 'O.K. but you did not answer my question, does it annoy you because you do it, or because I am saying that you do it?'

Avner: 'It is not because we are doing it, it is because this comparison is totally out of place.'

Nasser: 'Everyone has the right to understand things the way he wants. This is the way I feel, and there is nothing that can be done.'

Avner: 'Why do you compare it to the Holocaust?'

Nasser: 'I compare the two because I think that it is a Holocaust.'

This discussion was conducted at the intergroup level. Each group spoke in the first person and had its own 'truth'. The statements made were general, rational, abstract arguments or rhetorical questions. The students used this style of speech because it was clear to each side what the 'correct' answer was. No one tried to pose questions in order to get information. Both sides were entrenched in their positions. This style of collective talking generates a discourse in which the differences and distances between the groups are dominant. Increasing disconnection could be detected, a reaching of a dead end, and an inability or resistance to understanding the other group.

Discussions of the Holocaust and Al-Nakba in the university meetings took place, then, at a macro level. There was no mention of personal stories nor expression of personal feelings which might have evoked identification, empathy and, perhaps, a possibility of finding a common point of contact.

In Frankfurt, the topic of the Holocaust came up both before and after the visit to Buchenwald concentration camp. The joint visit of Jews and Arabs to a German concentration camp was a unique experience, unconventional in encounters between such groups. Before it took place, a dispute arose between the initiator, Sagy, the facilitators and the students. The Arabs argued that this visit violated the power balance between the two groups, arguing that:

Hassan (Arab male): 'The places that we are going to visit – the Anne Frank Museum, a concentration camp – I have the feeling of, 'What are we doing here?'

(Arab facilitator) 'The issue of the Holocaust is very difficult. I also have a problem with the visit, and we had an argument about it. The Arabs are in a tough situation. When the Jews are in Germany, the Holocaust takes up all the space, and the pain of the Arabs is pushed aside. It does not matter what you will do, there is a feeling that the Holocaust and the pain of the Jews is the issue.'

Other views were heard too:

Samira (Arab female): 'I do not have anything against the visit because I want to understand where it comes from. Because when I understand the pain of the other side, I expect that the Jewish side should understand my pain and my suffering. And I expect from myself to understand the other side, but this should not legitimise my oppression. The Holocaust caused the Jews to come and establish the state. I see a connection between the Holocaust and my oppression.'

The anticipated visit to the camp increased the the Arab participants' feelings of asymmetry. The setting in Frankfurt had already created the beginning of a different discourse to the one that had typified the University workshops. In the discussion that took place before the visit, the balance between group identity and individuals had already changed. There was a noticeable attempt on the part of the participants to separate themselves somewhat from the strict group emphasis and to grope for a more personal approach. For example:

Samir (Arab male): 'Yesterday I had a very heavy feeling, because I feel that whenever the Holocaust is approached, you close up. I don't know how to explain to you how I feel. Each time I tried to understand the Holocaust, it reminds me of the last 50 years of the Arabs, that their lands are taken away...'

Lital (Jewish female): 'Perhaps instead of comparing your (plural) pain to the Holocaust, you can try to describe your own pain. Perhaps you can display your picture as it is ... Every attempt to discuss it using 'the nation' vis-à-vis a nation is doomed to failure. I want to hear from you, Samir, your personal story of being dispossessed from your land.'

Hassan (Arab male): 'I think that I will feel like a stranger in the concentration camp, because it is expected of me to sit and identify, not express my feelings.'

Lital: 'I feel that you don't share with me ... You are not expected to identify. I just want you to tell me how you feel.'

Hassan: 'I feel like a stranger, that there is no room for me.'

After the visit to Buchenwald, the discourse became much more personal, even though the topic of the discussion remained on the collective level. Exerpts from the discussion after the visit exemplify the difference:

Hannit (Jewish female): 'We experienced so many things. I feel that, on the one hand, I have developed so many friendships with Jews and Arabs. On the other hand, I had the feeling that I was not respected as a member of another nation. It hinders me from forming something very homogeneous.'

Nasser (Arab male): 'What do you mean by saying that you were not respected as a nation?'

Hannit: 'That place (Buchenwald) evoked strong feelings in me, and the conversation afterward. Your and Suha's (Arab female) question (about the connection between the Holocaust and Al-Nakba) did something to me. I felt that you could ask the questions one to one, and understand our feelings, and as human beings to experience the sensations. But you still pushed the conflict inside by force. It brought me to high levels of anger and frustration.'

Suha: 'What did my question (about the connection between the Holocaust and Al-Nakba) do to you?'

Livnat (Jewish female): (crying) 'I could not cope with the Jewish-Arab question at that place.'

Lital: 'It was like you did not let us be victims for a moment.'

Nasser: 'I will tell you what I felt and what I feel. Yesterday I asked a question, which should not annoy you. Yesterday I was surprised by what I felt. I attended a Jewish school. I thought that the Holocaust belonged to the Jews only. I was surprised that 80 per cent of the prisoners in Buchenwald were non-Jews. The Holocaust is not only of the Jews. It was easier for me to understand it through the 80 per cent and not through the Jews.'

Hannit: 'I understood your question as if you were asking if we, the Jews, can do to you things that were done to us by the Nazis.'

Suha: 'In the camp, I lost all my defenses and felt it like a human being. But when we left, I thought about all the Arabs who were killed, and this is how I could connect myself to it.'

Nasser: 'I try all the time to approach you, and you put up this barrier. I try to identify with a person by getting to his place. I try to identify by being a victim, but you don't let me...'

In contrast to the argumentation, rhetorical questions and slogans that characterised the University workshops, discussion in Frankfurt took the form of description, personal stories and, most of all, expressions of personal feelings. Every participant made a serious attempt to reach deeper at the personal as well as in-group and intergroup level. Their exploration was of a different nature. Questions were asked to obtain information, to understand the thoughts and feelings of the others – those belonging to the in-group and especially belonging to the other group. The students expressed honest feelings and displayed greater ability to understand those of others. The discussions did not necessarily lead to agreement but they were incisive, open and deep. The personal level of the discourse, however, did not divert the emphasis from the conflict between the two groups. The process that developed was a new one, in which the intergroup discussion, through integration with personal elements, attained a deeper level of analysis of these intensely sensitive topics.

Conclusion
This chapter set out to evaluate two kinds of intergroup encounters as a means for decreasing animosity and increasing the potential for coexistence between two cultures (majority and minority) living in one country. Our analysis centered around the balance between emphasis on the individual versus emphasis on the group. This is linked to the goal of the encounters. Is it to enhance the feeling of closeness and the development of personal relationships, deeper insights and empathy between people as individuals, on the micro level? Or do these encounters attempt to find solutions to the social-national conflict and ways for coping on the macro level? The two different goals dictate different kinds of group facilitation.

The facilitation in the University workshops stressed the macro-level goal. The workshop was seen as providing an opportunity to interact with the 'other' on the group level and strengthen group identity (Halabi and Sonnenschein, 1999). This kind of facilitation is based on the categorical approach of maintaining group salience in intergroup-encounters (Hewstone and Brown, 1986). There was a tendency to develop modes of communication between two opposing groups representing different collectives. This led to encounters characterised by argumentation and politically-based discussions, with a focus on the problem of relations between Jews and Arabs and the inequalities existing between them in Israel. Issues were presented as black and white. When participants expressed doubts, they were either ignored (by the facilitators) or opposed (by the participants, mainly from the Arab group). The result was a deep sense of stalemate.

On the emotional level, many participants had strong feelings of frustration and emotional distress both inside and outside the workshops (Shahar, 1999). On the cognitive level, participants often clung to extreme positions and 'regressed' to less flexible collective identity. They clearly identified the 'other' as being the embodiment of 'evil', and their own group, whether Jewish or Arab, as the 'victim'. These results can be seen as a regressive process that inhibited learning and personal coping. Discussion emphasising the collective group level made participants aware of their total inability to make significant changes at the macro level. Azar (1979) calls this 'structural victimisation'.

The events in Frankfurt presented participants with a new situation and generated different results. Whereas the situation during the University workshop stressed the collective self and group identity, the situation during the week in Frankfurt stressed the importance of the individual self and multiple identities of gender, regional identity, etc. The informal and spontaneous activities – such as socialising with and helping one another, arranging parties – evoked a strong identity of a varied self. This identity largely overshadowed the group identity. Moreover, personal identity enabled people who were not totally identified with the group position to express themselves in various ways. The collective self, however, continued to remain salient in light of the workshop's subject, the discussions and the visits, especially to Buchenwald. Interaction between the various components of the individual self and collective identities appears to have developed during this unique encounter.

This could possibly be explained in terms of the 'common in-group identity' (Gaertner *et al*, 1993) which developed during the week in Frankfurt. Gaertner *et al* (1993) claim that cooperative contact between groups decreases intergroup bias by transforming the cognitive representations of the intergroup encounter as be-tween two groups into an encounter of one inclusive group. According to group identity theory, this change in perceptions may improve intergroup relations with different motivational pro-cesses, such as mutual help, mutual experiences, a feeling of belonging to one inclusive group as opposed to seeing some as outsiders. In 1958, Sherif developed an approach of shared group identity that has mutual goals. His model presents a direct link between perceived interdependence and a decrease in intergroup conflict. However, we find the approach of Gaertner *et al* (1993), which stresses the indirect effect of cognitive representations in creating the new group identity, more suitable for our analysis.

Quotations from the questionnaires filled out after the Frankfurt encounter and from the participants' diaries, relate to the new group identity and the effect it had on the participants:

> 'The highlight of the week we spent together in Germany was the discovery that in spite of the former acquaintance between us, we got to know each other and we became one group, a group of friends. Looking back, I understand that the big achievement of this week in Germany was the ability to accept from the 'other', be-fore categorising him, real trust. And it is nice and fulfilling, and it turns out to also be possible.' *Dana (Jewish female)*

> 'It is one of the few times in my life that I could connect so deeply to a group of Jews as individuals.' *Fatma (Arab female)*

> 'I was excited because of the deep and meaningful relations that developed with the other side and the ability to treat the other as a human being and not according to what nationality he belongs to.' *Hannit (Jewish female)*

'One group developed and I call it multicultural. Yelling and arguing until you cry, but also singing together on the trains, dancing,
and when we get tired, falling asleep on each other's shoulder.'
Nasser (Arab male)

The new group identity that developed at the Frankfurt workshop
did not erase former group identities but it did make them less
rigid. This flexibility developed because the new group identity
could enable other multi-group identities such as gender and
community and so on to emerge. Specifically, it enabled the
unique personal identity to stand out.

As a result of this process, a different kind of discourse became
possible, which included expressions of feelings and emotions as
well as doubts and hesitation. There were deeper personal insights
into the conflict, less stereotypical perceptions of the 'other', and
a more complex perception of the situation.

Many of the issues touched upon in this chapter provide insight
into resolving conflicts between two distinct cultural groups. Some
will be especially relevant to those interested in confronting
Islamophobia.

Notes on Contributors

Pieter Batelaan (Netherlands)
Pieter Batelaan is the co-founder and past president of the International Association for Intercultural Education. He has been a teacher, teacher trainer and educational consultant for various governmental and international institutions. He is also co-editor-in-chief of the academic journal *Intercultural Education*. He recently served in the capacity of rapporteur to the Council of Europe for the project 'The religious dimension in intercultural education'.

Michele Bertani (Italy)
Michele Bertani currently works with the Centre for Intercultural Studies at Verona University and with CESTIM NGO (Verona). He conducts research on modern Islam working together with COSPE NGO (Florence) and the European Monitoring Centre on Racism and Xenophobia (EUMC, Vienna).

Irene Donohoue Clyne (Australia)
Dr. Irene Donohoue Clyne teaches cross-cultural communication at the University of Melbourne and is coordinator for Cross-cultural Ministry for the Anglican Diocese of Melbourne. Her research and teaching focuses on the education of ethnic minority children . Her recent work includes the Education of Muslims in Australia and the education needs of Southern Sudanese Refugees.

Maurice Irfan Coles (UK)
Maurice Irfan Coles is Chief Executive of the School Development Support Agency (SDSA), a largely self-funded organisation working in partnership with Leicester City Council, England. He has worked in race equality in education in schools and local authorities.

Barry van Driel, editor, (USA/Netherlands)

Barry van Driel is the Secretary General of the International Association for Intercultural Education and Editor-in-Chief of the academic journal *Intercultural Education*. He is also employed as a curriculum developer and teacher trainer at the Anne Frank House, Amsterdam. He is presently implementing multiple projects in the USA and Europe that focus on prejudice reduction, education in a multicultural society and human rights education.

Mouin Fahiraladin (Israel)

Mouin Fahiraladin is a lecturer at Kay College of Education, Beer-Sheva, Israel. He is the chair of 'Eran' – emotional help by telephone (S.O.S.).

Beth Finkelstein (USA)

Beth Finkelstein is the Assistant Programme Director for Education at the Tanenbaum Center for Interreligious Understanding, a non-sectarian, secular nonprofit organisation headquartered in New York City.

Amber Haque (USA/Malaysia)

Dr. Amber Haque is Associate Professor in the Department of Psychology, International Islamic University of Malaysia. He has published mainly in the areas of mental health and religious psychology. One of his chief interests is the psychology of Muslim minorities living in the West.

Dr. Yasemin Karakaşoğlu (Germany)

Dr. Yasemin Karakaşoğlu (1965) is Assistant Professor for Intercultural Education (Department for Education, University of Essen). Current research interests include: Educational careers and living conditions of migrant children in Germany, Islam as a part of multiculturalism in German schools, as well as the headscarf discussion in German schools.

J'Lein Liese (USA)

J'Lein Liese founded the Institute for Multicultural Success International and the Foundation for Global Leadership. J'Lein's work both nationally and internationally specialises in violence prevention/intervention, responding to trauma, crisis management and issues concerning diversity. J'Lein is presently working with the

South African government to support the implementation of the new Child Justice System.

Sigrid Luchtenberg (Germany)

Sigrid Luchtenberg is professor in the faculty of education at Essen University, Germany. Her research interests and publications cover German as a first, second or foreign language as well as multicultural education, multicultural communication, the multiculturalism discourse in the media, and citizenship education in a multicultural society.

Robin Richardson (UK)

Robin Richardson is co-director of the education consultancy, 'Insted' in the UK. He was Director of the Runnymede Trust for five years, during which he brought out a report on antisemitism '*A very light sleeper*' and one on Islamophobia. The follow-up – *Islamophobia* – was also published by Trentham Books.

Prof. Shifra Sagy (Israel)

Prof. Sagy is currently the chair of the Department of Education and also heads the Center for Enhancement in Education at Ben Gurion University of the Negev.

Fida Sanjakdar (Australia)

Fida Sanjakdar has taught in primary, secondary and tertiary sectors. She is currently completing her PhD at the University of Melbourne. Her research interests include developing and implementing culturally appropriate curricula.

Dr. Lorraine Sheridan (UK)

Lorraine Sheridan is a lecturer in psychology at the University of Leicester. Her PhD is on the psychology of stalking behaviour, and she has published on a range of harassment-related issues. Her primary research interests cover stalkers and their victims, celebrity worship, Islamophobia, and offender profiling

Dr. Shoshana Steinberg (Israel)

Dr. Shoshana Steinberg is a senior lecturer at Kay College of Education in Beer-Sheva. She is involved in peace education and research in the Israeli-Palestinian context.

References

Abdel-Halim, A. (1989) *Meeting needs of Muslim students in the Australian Education system: research project*, Northmead: NSW.

Aboud, F. E., and Fenwick, V. (1999) Exploring and Evaluating School-Based Interventions to Reduce Prejudice. *Journal of Social Issues*, 55(4), pp. 767-786.

Ahmed, A. (2003) *Islam under Siege: Living Dangerously in a Post-honor World*, Polity Press.

Ahmed, J. (1967) *Hundred Great Muslims*. Ferozsons (Pvt.) Ltd.: Lahore, Pakistan.

Al-Attas, S.N. (Ed) (1979) *Aims and Objectives of Muslim Education*. London, UK: Hodder and Stoughton.

Ali, Aminah I. (1998) *The Three Muslim Festivals*. Chicago: International Educational Foundation.

Allam, M., and Gritti, R. (2001) *Islam, Italia*. Milano: Guerini.

Allen, C., and Nielsen, J.S. (2002) *Summary report on Islamophobia in the EU after 11 September 2001*. European Monitoring Centre on Racism and Xenophobia. Vienna.

Al-Qaradawi, Y. (1960) *The lawful and prohibited in Islam*. Indianapolis: American Trust Publications.

Al-Romi, N.H. (2000) Muslims as a minority in the United States. *International Journal of Educational Research*, 33, pp. 631-638.

Al-Sadan, I.A. (1999) The Pedagogy of the Prophe', *Muslim Education Quarterly*, 16(2), pp. 5-18.

Amir, Y., and Ben-Ari, R. (1989) Enhancing intergroup relations in Israel: A differential approach. In: D.Bar-Tal, C. Graumann, A. Kruglanski and W. Srobe (Eds) *Stereotyping and prejudice: Changing conceptions* (pp. 243-257). New York: Springer.

Apple, M. (1990) *Ideology and Curriculum*, 2nd Edition. London: Routledge and Kegan Paul.

Apple, M. (1993) *The Politics of Official Knowledge*. NY: Routledge.

Ashraf, S.A. (1998) The concept of sex in Islam and sex education. *Muslim Education Quarterly*, 15 (2), pp. 37-43.

Azar, E. E. (1979) Peace amidst development: A conceptual agenda for conflict and peace research. *International Interactions*, 6, pp. 123-143.

Baldock, J. (1991) *Discrimination Against Muslim Australians*, Melbourne: World Conference on Religion and Peace.

Bar, H., and Eady, A. (1998) Education to cope with conflicts. In: E. Weiner (Ed), *The Handbook of Coexistence*. New York: The Continuum.

Bargal, D., and Bar, H. (1996) Kurt Lewin approach and encounters of Arab-Palestinian and Jewish youth in Israel. *Studies in Education*, 1, pp. 15-34. (Hebrew).

Bar-Tal, D., and Labin, D. (2001) The effects of a major event on stereotyping: terrorist attacks in Israel and Israeli adolescents' perceptions of Palestinians, Jordanians and Arabs. *European Journal of Social Psychology*, 31, pp. 265-280.

Batelaan, P. (2003) *Intercultural education and the challenge of religious diversity and dialogue in Europe*. Strasbourg: Council of Europe, Steering Committee for Education, DG IV/EDU/DIAL, 1 Rev.

Batelaan, P., and Gundara, J. (1993) Cultural Diversity and the promotion of Values through Education. *European Journal of Intercultural Studies*, 3 (2/3).

Bauer, T., Kaddor, L., and Strobel, K. (Eds) (2004) *Islamischer Religionsunterricht: Hintergründe, Probleme, Perspektiven*. Münster: LIT.

Beckett, L., (1996) Where do you draw the line?: Education and Sexual Identities. In: Laskey, L., and Beavis, C. (Eds), *Schooling and Sexualities. Victoria, Deakin Centre for Education and Change*, Deakin University.

Behr, H. H., Bochinger, C., and Klinkhammer, G. (2003) *Perspektiven für die Ausbildung muslimischer Religionslehrerinnen und Religionslehrer in Deutschland*. Eine Expertise. Kulturwissenschaftliche Fakultät Universität Karlsruhe.

Berkowitz, L. (1989) Frustration-aggression hypothesis: Examination and reformulation. *Psychological Bulletin*, 106, pp. 59-73.

Berkowitz, L. (1990) On the formation and regulation of anger and aggression: A cognitive neo-associationistic analysis. *American Psychologist*, 45, pp. 494-503.

Bennett, T. (1992) Putting policy into cultural studies. In: Grossberg, L., Nelson, C. and Treichler, P.A. (Eds), *Cultural Studies*, NY: Routledge.

Berns McGown, R. (1999) *Muslims in the Diaspora: the Somali communities of London and Toronto*. Toronto: University of Toronto Press.

Blaschke, J., and Sabanovic, S., (2000) Multi-Level Discrimination of Muslim Women in Germany. In: Blaschke, Jochen (Ed): *Multi-Level Discrimination of Muslim Women in Europe*, Berlin 2000, pp. 37-55.

Brady, L., and Kennedy, K. (1999) *Curriculum Construction*. Sydney: Prentice Hall.

Brodribb, T. (1981) *Manual of Health and Temperance*. Melbourne, Victorian Programme of Instruction, Victorian Education Department.

Buckley, S. (1987) The struggle for Nur. *Insight*, 2 (1), pp. 24-25.

Buckley, S. (1991) *Bridges of Light: the struggle of an Islamic private school in Australia*. Lakemba, N.S.W: The Muslim Service Association.

Bullivant, B.M. (1981) *Race, Ethnicity and Curriculum*. Melbourne: The Macmillan Company of Australia.

Burchill, J. (2001) *The Guardian*, 18 September.

Cahill, D et al. (1996) *Immigration and schooling in the 1990s*, Canberra: Department of Immigration and Ethnic Affairs, AGPS.

Cameron, J. A., Alvarez, J. M., Ruble, D. M., and Fuligni A. J. (2001) Children's Lay Theories About Ingroups and Outgroups: Reconceptualizing Research on Prejudice. *Personality and Social Psychology Review*, 5(2), pp. 118-128.

Carroll, B., and Hollinshead, G. (1993), Ethnicity and Conflict in Physical Education. *British Educational Research Journal*, 19(1), pp. 59-75.

Clancy, A., Hough, M., Aust, R., and Kershaw, C. (2001) *Crime, policing and justice: The experience of ethnic minorities – findings from the British Crime Survey.* Home Office Research Study 223. London: HMSO.

Collins, C. (2002) The content of the curriculum: What will Young Australians be Learning. *Curriculum Perspectives*, 22 (1), pp. 44-49.

Colquhoun, D., Goltz, K., and Sheehan, M. (1997) *The Health Promoting School: Policy, Programmes and Practice in Australia.* Melbourne: Harcourt Brace and Company.

Conway, G (1997) Preface. Runnymede Commission on British Muslims and Islam. London: UK.

Council on American-Islamic Relations (2004) *Anti-Muslim Incidents Jump 70 per cent in 2003.* Washington D.C.: CAIR-Council on American-Islamic Relations.

Council on American-Islamic Relations (2004) *Florida Muslim Child Assaulted in School.* Washington D.C.: CAIR-Council on American-Islamic Relations.

Council on American-Islamic Relations (2003) *Florida Muslim Students Kicked Off Bus 5 Miles from Home.* Washington D.C.: CAIR-Council on American-Islamic Relations.

Council on American-Islamic Relations (2004) *Louisiana Teacher Removed After Hijab Incident.* Washington D.C.: CAIR-Council on American-Islamic Relations.

Council on American-Islamic Relations Research Center (2002) *The Status of Muslim Civil Rights in the United States 2002: Stereotypes and Civil Liberties.* Washington D.C.: CAIR-Council on American-Islamic Relations.

Cross, S. (1983) *Catch them as they go: religious change in Australia,* (videorecording) Sydney NSW: Argosy Films for Network 0/28.

Currie, C., Todd, J. and Thomson, C. (1997) *Health Behaviours of Scottish School-children: Report 6: Sex Education, Personal Relationships, Sexual Behaviour and HIV/AIDS Knowledge and Attitudes in 1990 and 1994.* RUHBC and HEBS, Edinburgh.

Davis, D., and Butler, T. (1996) *Health and Physical Education, Book 2.* National Library of Australia: Macmillan.

Department of Employment, Education, Training and Youth Affairs (1997) *Schools Funding: consultation report.* Canberra: AGPS.

Deutsche Shell (Ed)(2000) *13. Shell-Jugendstudie. Jugend 2000,* Opladen.

Dewan, S. K. (2003) Muslim Girl Punched in Face: Boy is Arrested. *New York Times* Metro Section, 17 September 2003.

DFES (2004) *The curriculum reflecting the experiences of African Caribbean and Muslim pupils.*

Doise, W., Deschamps, J.C., and Meyer, G. (1978) The accentuation of intra-category similarities. In: H. Tajfel (Ed), *Differentiation between social groups,* London: Academic Press.

Donohoue Clyne, I. (1997a) Those preaching tolerance fail to extend it to Islamic schools. *The Age* January 8th pA11.

Donohoue Clyne, I. (1997b) Seeking Education for Muslim children in Australia. *Muslim Education Quarterly,* 14(3), pp. 4-18.

Donohoue Clyne, I. (1998) Cultural diversity and the curriculum: the Muslim experience in Australia, *European Journal of Intercultural Education,* 9(3), pp. 279-289.

Donohoue Clyne, I. (1999) Funding Islamic schools: the debate and the decisions, In: F. Clyne and R.R. Woock, (Eds) *Culture, Crisis and Education: comparative perspectives for the new millennium*. Melbourne: Faculty of Education/Youth Research Centre of The University of Melbourne.

Donohoue Clyne, I. (2000) Seeking Education: the struggle of Muslims to educate their children in Australia. Unpublished PhD thesis University of Melbourne.

Donohoue Clyne, I. (2001) Educating Muslim Children in Australia, In: Saeed, A. and Akbarzadeh S (Eds) *Muslim Communities in Australia*, Sydney: University of NSW Press.

Donohoue Clyne, I. (2003a) 'Muslim Women: some western fictions' in Jawaard, H. and Benn T. (Eds) *Muslim Women in the West*, The Netherlands: Brill.

Donohoue Clyne, I. (2003b) The role of parents in the learning organisation: Muslim parents' discourse on curriculum, paper presented at Annual Conference of ATEE, University of Malta, Valetta Malta. August 24-27th.

Donohoue Clyne, I. (2003c) Education and Islamic Identity in Australia, paper presented at *Perspectives on Islam Workshop*, University of South Australia, Adelaide Nov 28-9th.

Dovidio, J.F., and Fazio, R.H. (1991) New technologies for the direct and indirect assessment of attitudes. In: J.M. Tanur (Ed). *Questions about survey questions: meaning, memory, attitudes and social interaction*. (pp. 204-237). New York: Russell Sage Foundation.

D'Oyen, F.M. (1996) *The Miracle of Life: A Guide on Islamic Family Life and Sex Education for Young People*. Leicester: Islamic Foundation.

Dunn, K. (2003) Attitudes towards immigration and immigrants: a) perspectives. Findings of a survey on racist attitudes and experiences of racism in Australia. Paper presented to the conference *New Directions: New Settlers: New Challenges*, Wellington, Australia.

Durkee, N (1987) Primary Education of Muslim Children in North America, *Muslim Education Quarterly*, 5(1).

Dwyer, C. and Meyer, A. (1996) The establishment of Islamic schools: a controversial phenomenon in three European countries, In: W.A.R. Shadid and P.S. Van Koningsveld (Eds) *Muslims in the margin: political responses to the presence of Islam in Western Europe*. Kampen, The Netherlands: Kok Pharos Publishing House.

Eck, D. L. (2001) *A New Religious America*. San Francisco: Harper Collins.

Eisner, E.W. (1994) *The Educational Imagination: On the Design and Evaluation of School Programmes* 3rd Edition. NY: McMillan College Publishing Company.

Epstein, D., and Johnson, R. (1998) *Schooling Sexualities*. Buckingham: Open University Press.

Eslea, M., and Mukhtar, K. (2000) Bullying and racism among Asian schoolchildren in Britain. *Educational Research*, 42, pp. 207-217.

Esses, V., Haddock, G., and Zanna, M.P. (1994) The Role of Mood in the Expression of Intergroup Stereotypes. In: *The Psychology of Prejudice: The Ontario Symposium Volume 7*. New Jersey: Lawrence Erlbaum Associates, Inc., pp. 77-103.

European Monitoring Centre on Racism and Xenophobia (2002a) *Anti-Islamic reactions in the EU after the terrorist act against the USA. A collection of country reports from RAXEN National Focal Points (NFPs)*, Germany, European Forum for Migration Studies, Vienna.

European Monitoring Centre on Racism and Xenophobia (2002b) *Summary Report on Islamophobia in the EU after 11 September 2001*, Vienna.

Farley, R.R. (2000) Sociological Perspectives: The Order and Conflict Models. In: Farley (Ed) *Majority-Minority Relations*, 4th ed., pp. 69-101.

Fouad Allam, K. (2002) *L'islam globale*. Milano: Rizzoli.

Finklestein, B. (2003) *Presentation at New York University, Steinhardt School of Education* 19 November 2003.

Fullan, M. (2001) *Leading in a Culture of Change*. Jossey-Bas.

Gaertner, S., Dovidio, J., Anastasio, P., Bachman, B., and Rust, M. (1993) The common ingroup identity model: Recategorization and the reduction of intergroup bias. In: W. Stroebe and M. Hewstone (Eds) *European Review of Social Psychology*. (Vol. 4), pp. 1-26). Chichester: Wiley.

Garbarino, J. (1999) *Lost Boys: Why our sons turn violent and how we can save them*. New York: Anchor Books.

Giroux, H.A. (1981) *Ideology, Culture and the Process of schooling*. UK: Temple University Press.

Green, B. (2003) Curriculum Inquiry in Australia: Toward a Local Genealogy of the curriculum field. In: Pinar, W.F (Ed) *International Handbook of Curriculum Research*. Mahwah, N.J: Erlbaum Associates.

Grundy, S. (1987) *Curriculum: Product or Praxis*. London: Falmer Press.

Guardian Newspaper, April 19th 2003.

Guerrera, O., and Jackson, A. (2003) Minister urges watch on Islamic schools. *The Age* March 28th p4.

Guolo, R. (2003) *Xenofobil e Xenofili. I rapporti con l'Islam*: il rischio Italianistan.

Gundara, J. S. (2000) *Interculturalism, Education and Inclusion*. London: Paul Chapman.

Haddad, Y.Y. (1991) *The Muslims of America*. New York: Oxford University Press.

Halabi, R., and Sonnenschein, N. (1999) The work approach at the School for Peace. Unpublished manuscript. Neve Shalom the School for Peace.

Halstead, J. M. (1986a) To what extent is the call for separate Muslim voluntary-aided schools in the U.K. justified? Part 1, *Muslim Education Quarterly*, 3(2), pp.5-26.

Halstead, J. M. (1986b) To what extent is the call for separate Muslim voluntary-aided schools in the U.K. justified? Part 2, *Muslim Education Quarterly*, 3(3), pp.3-40.

Halstead, J.M. (1997) Muslims and Sex education. *Muslim Education Quarterly*, 26(3), pp. 317-330.

Halstead, J.M., and Lewicka, K. (1998) Should Homosexuality be taught as an acceptable alternative lifestyle? A Muslim perspective. *Cambridge Journal of Education*, 28(1), pp. 49-64.

Halstead, J.M., and Reiss, M.J. (2003) *Values in Sex education: From Principles to Practice*. London: Routledge Falmer.

Hargreaves, A. (1995) Changing Teachers, *Changing times – teacher's work and culture in the postmodern age*. London: Cassell.

Hatton, E. (1998) Understanding Teaching. In: Hatton, E. (Ed) *Understanding Teaching*, 2nd Edition. Sydney: Harcourt Brace.

Haw, K.K. (1998) *Educating Muslim Girls: Shifting Discourses*. p. 58, Open University Press.

Hayes, C. C., and Thomas, O. (2001) *Finding Common Ground: A Guide to Religious Liberty in Public Schools*. Nashville TN: First Amendment Center.

Helms, J. (Ed) (1990) *Black and white radical identity*. Greenwood Press.

Henzell-Thomas, J. (2002) *The Challenge of Pluralism and the Middle Way of Islam*, Association of Muslim Social Scientists.

Hermans, P. (in press) Applying Ogbu's Theory of Minority Academic Achievement to the Situation of Moroccans in the Low Countries. *Intercultural Education*, 15(3).

Hewstone, M., and Brown, R.J. (1986) Contact is not enough: an intergroup perspective on the contact hypothesis. In: M. Hewstone and R.J. Brown (Eds) *Contact and conflict in intergroup encounters* (pp. 1-44). Oxford: Blackwell.

Hippler, J., and Lueg, A. (Eds) (1995) *The next threat: western perceptions of Islam*. London, UK: Pluto Press.

Hitchens, P. (2002) Mail on Sunday, 27 October. The discussion that follows here is drawn from *Islamophobia: issues, challenges and action*.

Hoffman, M. (2000) *Islam the Alternative*. Suhail Academy: Lahore, Pakistan.

Hofstede, G. (1986) Cultural Differences in Teaching and Learning *International Journal of Inter-Cultural Relations*,10, pp. 301-320.

Hulmes, E. (1989) *Education and Cultural Diversity*. London UK: Longman.

Hussain, A., and Hussain, I. (1996) A brief history and demographics of Muslims in the United States. In: Asad Husain, John Woods and Javed Akhtar (Eds). *Muslims in America: Opportunities and Challenges*. Chicago: International Strategy and Policy Institute.

Irvine, J.M. (1995) *Sexuality Education Across Cultures: Working with Differences*. San Francisco: Jossey-Bass Publishers.

Kanpol, B. (1989) Do we dare teach some truths? An argument for teaching more 'hidden curriculum'. *College Student Journal*, 23(3): pp. 214-217.

Karakaşoğlu, Y. (1996) Turkish Cultural Orientations in Germany and the Role of Islam. In: Horrocks, David and Kolinsky, Eva (Ed) *Turkish Culture in German Society Today*, Oxford, pp. 157-179.

Karakaşoğlu, Y. (2003) Custom Tailored Islam: Second generation female students of Turko-Muslim origin in Germany and their concept of religiousness in the light of modernity and education. In: Sackmann, R., Faist, Th., and Peters, B. (Eds): *Identity and Integration. Migrants in Western Europe*, Ashgate, London, pp. 107-226.

Katz, I., and Kahanof, M. (1990) A survey of dilemmas in moderating Jewish Arab encounter groups in Israel. *Megamot*, 33, pp. 29-47 (Hebrew).

Kazi, M.U. (1992) *A Treasury of Ahadith*, Jeddah, Saudi Arabia, Abdul- Quasim Publishing House.

Keane, J. (2003) Power Sharing Islam? In: A. Tamimi's *Power Sharing Islam?* Pp. 16-16. Institute of Islamic Political Thought: London, UK.

Kelly, E. (2004) Integration, Assimilation and Social Inclusion: questions of faith. *Policy Futures in Education*, 2(1).

Kilroy Silk, R. (2004) *Sunday Express*, 4 January.

Kimmerling, B.(1999) Al-Nakba. In: A., Ophir (Ed) *Fifty to forty-eight: Critical moments in history of the State of Israel.* Jerusalem: The Van Leer Institute. (Hebrew).

Kirk, D., and Tinning, R. (1990) Introduction: Physical Education Curriculum and Culture. In: Kirk, D. and Tinning, R. (Eds) *Physical Education Curriculum and Culture: Critical Issues in the Contemporary Crisis,* London: The Falmer Press.

Lang, J (1996) *Even Angels Ask: A Journey to Islam in America.* pp. 230. Beltsville: MD, Amana Publications.

Lavin, A.T., Shapiro, G. R., and Weill, K.S. (1992) Creating an agenda for school based health promotion: A review of 25 selected reports. *Journal of School Health,* 62(6), pp. 212-228.

Leeds, A. (2004) *Presentation at East Moriches Elementary School* 26 April 2004.

Leibold, J., and Kühnel, S. (2003) 'Islamophobie. Sensible Aufmerksamkeit für spannungsreiche Anzeichen. In: Heitmeyer, Wilhelm (Ed): *Deutsche Zustände,* Frankfurt am Main: Suhrkamp, pp. 100-120.

Lemmen, T., and Miehl, M. (2002) *Islamisches Alltagsleben in Deutschland.* Bonn: Friedrich-Ebert-Stiftung, 2nd edition.

Lindsay, K., McEwan, S., and Knight, J. (1987) Islamic Principles and Physical Education. *Unicorn,* 13(2), pp. 75-78.

Logan, G.C. (1980) *Sex education in Queensland, a history of the debate 1900-1980.* Queensland, Queensland Department of Education.

Lovat T.J., and Smith, D.L. (2003) *Curriculum: action on reflection revisited,* 4th Edition. Wentworth Falls Australia: Social Science Press.

Mabud, S.A. (1998) An Islamic view of sex education. *The Muslim Education Quarterly,* 15(2), pp. 67- 93.

Malik, N. (2001) Religious discrimination: historical and current developments in the English legal system. *Encounters,* 7, pp. 57-78.

Margolis, E., and Romero, M. (1998) 'The department is very male, very white, very old, and very conservative': The functioning of the hidden curriculum in graduate sociology departments. *Harvard Educational Review,* 68(1): pp. 1-32.

Markus, H.R., and Kitayama, S. (1991) Culture and the self: Implications for cognition, emotion, and motivation. *Psychological Review,* 98, pp. 224-253.

Marsella, A., De Vos, G., and Hsu, F.L.K. (1985) *Culture and Self.* London: Tavistock.

Marsh, C., and Willis, G. (1999) *Curriculum: Alternative Approaches, Ongoing Issues.* Sydney: Prentice Hall.

Maslen, G. (1982) *School Ties: private schooling in Australia.* North Ryde NSW: Methuen Australia Pty. Ltd.

McGee, C. (1997) *Teachers and Curriculum Decision Making.* New Zealand: Dunmore Press.

McInerney, D. M., Davidson, N., and Suliman, R. (2000) Personal Development, Health and Physical Education in context: Muslim and Catholic perspectives. *Australian Journal of Education,* 44(1), pp. 26-42.

McKay, A. (1997) Accommodating Ideological pluralism in sexuality education. *Journal of Moral Education,* 26(3), pp. 285-300.

McNeil, J.D. (2003) *Curriculum: The Teacher's Initiative,* 3rd Edition. NJ: Upper Saddle River.

Michaelsen, R. (1970) *Piety In The Public School.* London: Macmillian Company.

Ministry of Education (1980) *Report of the advisory committee on Health and Human Relationship Education in schools to the Honourable Norman Lacy, MP* Assistant Minister of Education.

Ministry of Education, (schools division) Victoria, (1989) *The Personal Development Framework: P-10*, State Government Printers.

Mortensen, K. G. (1985) *Politics and Sociology of Funding Australian Schools*, Parkville, Victoria: Gerald Griffin Press.

Muslim Council of Britain (2002) *The Quest for Sanity: Reflections on September 11 and the Aftermath.* pp. 198-201.

Nahdi, F. (2001) Quoted in *The Guardian*, 24 September.

Nahdi, F. (2003) Young, British and Ready to Fight, *The Guardian*, 1 April.

Nahdi, F. (2003) Tel Aviv First, Then Manchester?, *The Guardian*, 2 May.

Nasr, S.H. (1983) *Science and Civilization in Islam.* Suhail Academy: Lahore, Pakistan.

New South Wales Education Department (1984) *Health Studies* (K-12), New South Wales Education Department.

Noibi, D. O. (1998) The Islamic concept of sex, sexuality and sex education: A theological perspective. *Muslim Education Quarterly*, 15(2), pp. 44- 67.

Nord, W. A., and Haynes, C. C. (1998) *Taking Religion Seriously Across the Curriculum.* Alexandria, VA: Association for Supervision and Curriculum Development.

Nutbeam, D., Wise, M., Bauman, A., Harris, E., and Leeder, S. (1993) *Goals and Targets for Australia's Health in the year 2000 and Beyond.* Canberra: AGPS.

Nyang, S.S. (1999) *Islam in the United States of America.* Chicago: ABC International Group, Inc.

Oakes, J. (1985) *Keeping track: How schools structure inequality.* New Haven, Connecticut: Yale University Press.

Ollis, D., and Mitchell, A. (1999) *Talking sexual health: National framework for education about HIV/AIDS, STDs and Blood Borne Viruses in secondary schools.* Canberra: Australian National Committee on AIDS and Related diseases.

Omeish, M.S. (1999) Muslim students' perceptions of prejudice and discrimination in American academia: Challenges, issues and obstacles and the implications for educators, administrators and university officials. *Dissertation Abstracts International: Section A: Humanities and Social Sciences*, 60, 2-A, 0360.

Oxford English Dictionary (1994) Oxford: Oxford University Press.

Oyserman, D. (1993) The lens of personhood: Viewing the self and others in a multicultural society. *Journal of Personality and Social Psychology*, 65, pp. 993-1009.

Pace, E. (1999) *Sociologia dell'islam.* Roma: Carocci editore.

Pallotta-Chiarolli, M. (1996) A Rainbow in my Heart: Interweaving ethnicity and sexuality studies. In: Laskey, L., and Beavis, C. (Eds) *Schooling and Sexualities Victoria.* Deakin Centre for Education and Change, Deakin University, Victoria.

Parekh report (2000) *The Future of Multi-Ethnic Britain*, Profile Books.

Partington, G., and McCudden, V. (1992) *Ethnicity and Education.* Australian Social Science Press.

Pew Forum on Religion and Public Life (2003) *Pew Forum Updates: Week of 7-24-03* Washington D.C.: Pew Forum.

Phinney, J.S. (1990) Ethnic identity in adolescents and adults: Review of research. Psychological Bulletin, 108, pp. 499-514.

Piccardo, H. R. (1999) *L'islam nella scuola, in La visione della multiculturalità*, I. Sigillino (a cura di), Milano: Franco Angeli.

Portera, A. (a cura di), (2003) Educazione e pedagogia interculturale. *Pedagogia interculturale in Italia e in Europa*. Milano: Vita e Pensiero.

Posner, G.J. (1995) *Analyzing the Curriculum*. NY: McGraw Hall.

Pulcini, T. (1990) A Lesson in Values Conflict: Issues in the Educational Formations of American Muslim Youth, *Journal Institute of Muslim Minority Affairs*, 11(1), pp.127-152.

Print, M. (1993) *Curriculum Development and Design*, Australia, Ullen and Unwin.

Ramadan, T. (1999) *To be European Muslim*, The Islamic Foundation.

Ramadan, T. (2002) *Essere musulmano europeo*. Enna: Città Aperta.

Raza, M. S.(1993) *Islam in Britain Past, Present and Future*. Volcano Press.

Reid, A. (2002) Point and counterpoint: Features of Australian Curriculum. *Curriculum Perspectives*, 22(1), pp. 43-44.

Reiss, M.J., and Mabud, S.A. (1998) *Sex Education and Religion*. UK: The Islamic Academy.

Rouhana, N. R., and Korper, S. H. (1997) Power asymmetry and goals of unofficial third party intervention in protracted intergroup conflict. *Peace and Conflict: Journal of Peace Psychology*, 3, pp. 1-17.

Ruenzel, D. (1996) Old-Time Religion. *Education Week*, 15 (27).

Runnymede Trust (1997) *Islamophobia: A challenge for us all*. London: Runnymede Trust.

Sagy, S. (2000) Myself in society and society in myself. In: D. Bar-On (Ed), *Bridging the Gap*. Hamburg: Korber Foundation edition.

Sagy, S., Orr, E., Bar-On, D. and Awwad, E. (2001) Individualism and collectivism in two conflicted societies: Comparing Israeli and Palestinian high school students. *Youth and Society*, 32, pp. 3-30.

Sahadat, J. (1997) Islamic Education: A challenge to Conscience. *The American Journal of Islamic Social Sciences*, 14(4), pp. 19-34.

Saint-Blancat, C. (1997) *L'islam della diaspora*. Roma: Edizioni Lavoro.

Saint-Blancat, C. (a cura di) (1999) *L'islam in Italia. Una presenza plurale*. Roma: Edizioni Lavoro.

Sanjakdar, F. (2000) A study of the hidden and core curriculum of an Islamic school, M.Ed thesis (unpublished), University of Melbourne, Australia.

Sanjakdar, N (2000) Why do Muslim parents choose King Khalid Islamic College of Victoria? M.Ed thesis (unpublished), University of Melbourne, Australia.

Sarwar, G. (1996) *Sex Education: The Muslim Perspective*, 3rd Edition. UK: The Muslim Education Trust.

Saylor, J.G., Alexander, W.M., and Lewis, A.J., (1981) *Curriculum Planning for better teaching and learning*, 4th Edition. NY: Holt, Rinehart and Winston.

Sears, J.T (1997) Centering Culture: Teaching for critical sexual literacy using the sexual diversity wheel. *Journal of Moral Education*, 26(3), pp. 273-283.

Shahar, G. (1999) *The politics of emotional distress in Jewish-Arab group.* Annual report of the School for Peace. Neve Shalom / Wahat al Salam.

Shamma, F. (1999) The curriculum challenge for Islamic schools in America. In: A. Haque (Ed), *Muslims and Islamization in North America.* Beltsville, MD: Amana Publishers.

Shboul, A. (1984) Is Islam misunderstood in Australia? In: M. Humphrey and A. Mograby (Eds) *Islam in Australia, Proceedings of seminar held at McArthur Institute of Higher Education,* Middle East Research and Information Service/NSW Anti-Discrimination Board: Sydney Australia.

Sirozi, M. (2004) Secular-religious debates on the Indonesian national education system: Colonial legacy and a search for national identity in education. *Intercultural education.*

Smith A., Agius, P., Dyson, S., Mitchell, A., and Pitts, M., (2003) Results of the 3rd *National Survey of Australian Secondary Students, HIV/AIDS and Sexual Health, 2002* Melbourne, Australian Research Centre in Sex, Health and Society, LaTrobe University.

Smith, T. W. (2002) *Religious Diversity in America.* New York: American Jewish Committee.

Sonnenschein, N., Halabi, R., and Friedman, A. (1998) Israeli-Palestinian workshops: Legitimation of national identity and change in power relationships. In: G. Weiner (Ed), *The handbook of coexistence.* (pp. 600-614). New York: the continuum.

Suleiman, R. (1996) Planned encounters between Jew and Palestinian Israelis: A Social-psychological perspective. *Studies in Education,* 1, pp.71-81. (Hebrew).

Tanenbaum Center for Interreligious Understanding (2004) *Eid Ul-Fitr in Jordan.* New York NY: Tanenbaum Center for Interreligious Understanding.

Thomson, R. (Ed) (1993) *Religion, Ethnicity and Sex education: Exploring the issues, A Resource for teachers and others working with young people.* London: Sex Education Forum.

Triandis, H.C. (1989) The self and social behaviour in differing cultural contexts. *Psychological Review,* 96, pp. 506-520.

Turbes, S., Krebs, E., and Axtel, S. (2002) The hidden curriculum in multicultural medical education: The role of case examples. *Academic Medicine,* 77(3): pp. 209-216.

Ulanowsky, C. (1998) Sex education: Beyond information to values. *Muslim Education Quarterly,* 15(2), pp. 15- 23.

Vercellin, G. (2000) *Tra veli e turbanti; Rituali sociali e vita privata nei mondi dell'Islam.* Venezia: Marsilio Editori.

von Hirsch, A. (1996) *Beliefs and ideas concerning childhood and childrearing: a study of Christian and Arab speaking families at Raby,* Västerås: Westerås Media Tryck AB.

von Wilamowitz-Moellendorff, U. (2003) *Was halten die Deutschen vom Islam? Ergebnisse einer Umfrage,* (Ed) Konrad-Adenauer-Stiftung e.V., Arbeitspapiere/Dokumentationen No. 109, Sankt Augustin.

Walker, D.F, (2003) *Fundamentals of curriculum: passion and professionalism.* Mahwah, N.J.: Lawrence Erlbaum Associates.

Weller, P., Feldman, A., and Purdam. K. (2001) *Religious discrimination in England and Wales.* Home Office Research Study 220. London: HMSO.

Werribee Islamic College Inc. (1996) *The Islamic Schools of Victoria,* Information Brochure for Parents.

Wingfield, M., and Karaman, B. (1995) *Arab Stereotypes and American Educators.* Dearborn MI: American-Arab Anti-Discrimination Committee.

Wolcott, I. (1987) *Human Relations Education in Australian Schools: A review of Policies and Practices.* Melbourne: Australian Institute of Family Studies.

Wright, P. (1992) *Inside and out: A health and physical education workbook.* ACHPER Australia: Jacaranda.

Zaman, M. O. (2002) *The Ulama in Contemporary Islam: Custodians of Change.* Princeton and Oxford.

Zawadzki, B. (1948) Limitations on the scapegoat theory of prejudice. *Journal of Abnormal and Social Psychology,* 43, pp.127-141.

Zincone, G. (a cura di) (2001) *Secondo rapporto sull'integrazione degli immigrati in Italia.* Bologna: Il Mulino

Web references

Anti-Defamation League http://www.adl.org

Burke, K. – Divided we stand- on the street and in the playground, The Sydney Morning Herald, June 24th, also: www.smh.com.au/articles/2003/06/23/10562205 42336.html

Council on American-Islamic Relations. Muslim Community Safety Kit. http://www.cair-net.org

DawaNet – American Muslim History. http://www.dawanet.co,/history/amermuslim hist.asp

Doherty, L. – Blow out in private school aid Sydney Morning Herald June 24th http://www.smh.com.au/articles/2003/06/23/10566220542348.html

Encarta Dictionary http://encarta.msn.com/dictionary_/slur.html

Hassani S. – One Thousand Years of Muslim History. www.Muslimheritage. com

Karvelas, P. – Muslim School Of Hard Knocks The Australian Sept. 10th http://www.theaustralian.news.com.au

Maiden, S. – Funding Favours Islamic Schools, The Australian Jan. 9th www.theaustralian.com.au/printpage/0,5942/8352556.00.html

Minaret College 2004 www.minaret.vic.edu.au

Morris, L. – Islam leads in rush to faith education, Sydney Morning Herald June 23rd. www.smh.com.au/text/articles/2003/06/22/1056220477178.htm

MuslimHeritage.com http://www.muslimheritage.com/day_life/default.cfm

Muslim Scientists and Scholars http://www.ummah.net/history/scholars/

National Conference for Community and Justice http://www.nccj.org

Project MAPS – Results of Poll of American Muslims. Georgetown University. http://communications.georgetown.edu/press_releases/122001/maps_ study.html

Runnymede Trust – Islamophobia a Challenge for Us All. www.sdsa.net

Southern Poverty Law Center's Mix it Up project http://www.mixitup.org

Tamimi, A. Incriminating Islam-Islamophobia, p. 2. http://www.ii-pt.com/web/papers/incriminating.htm

Thought: London, UK. http://www.ii-pt.com/web/papers/incriminating.htm

Zogby International http://www.zogby.com/index.cfm